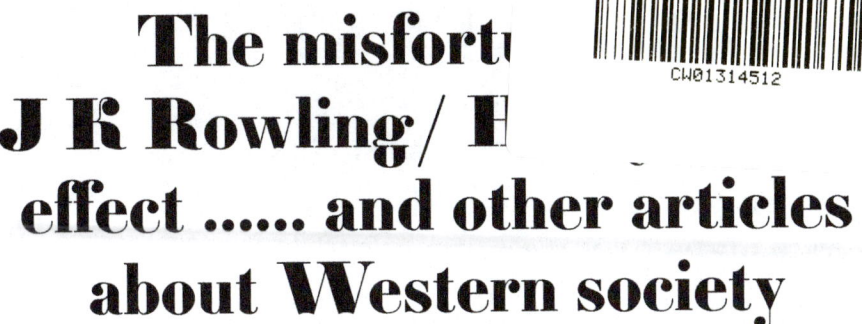

All rights reserved. No part of this work may be reproduced or stored in an information retrieval system (other than for purposes of review) without the express permission of the publisher in writing.

The right of G C Burnell to be identified as the author of this work has been asserted by him in accordance with the Copyright, Designs and Patents Act 1988

©Copyright 2023 G C Burnell

Published by Amory Publishing

To contact the publisher, in the first instance message them from their website.

To find out more about our other books, go to www.amorypublishing.co.uk

CONTENTS

SECTION 1
Articles on education and social studies

1) Fun as therapy	7
2) The need to fail	9
3) The misfortune of a J K Rowling/ Harry Potter effect	13
4) The bad news and the good news	15
5) Man may (basically) be a fighter – but against whom – or what?	17
6) Some readers are so widely read – but is it an asset?	21
7) About my experiences with the encounter group movement back in the 80s	23
8) Our instincts	27
9) How boring is our work	29
10) A good forgetery	31
11) Become an expert in something	32
12) The importance of the two week cooling off period – and its implications	34
13) Generalised insight therapy	39
14) When you're looking for a job, think of the perks	47
15) Choose hobbies that are 'unisex'	50
16) The healing power of (live) music	51
17) Bunn Leisure caravan site as a kind of 'model' – enjoying 'live' music rather than TV	58
18) Education (1)	68
19) Education (2)	76
20) Education (3)	78

SECTION 2
Hampshire journalism at the cutting edge

A large number of (mainly) small articles   81

SECTION 3
Being more reasonable in business

1) 3 examples of being 'unreasonable' in business	102
2) The secret of those "permanent half-price sales" – and more info on consuming to make one's blood boil!	109
3) About private equity firms	115
4) Heading towards authoritarianism and other negatives	119
5) Big vs small – as regards company size	125
6) The ludicrous housing situation	135
7) Why doesn't anyone go for a walk anymore?	141
8) Do you speak Japanese?	144
9) A suggestion for the government	146
10) Let's give singers and musicians who aren't famous a chance	148
11) Slaves to the Methodist work ethic – why many people work too hard	159

INTRODUCTION

As implied by the subtitle, this book is largely about overcoming repressed aggression. (And I have a 'sister book'*, also available at Amazon, which is mainly about overcoming sexual repression.) Repressed aggression and sexual repression were originally Freud's ideas – and very good ones too. I also accept Freud's idea that we have a sexual drive and an aggressive drive. In fact it's when there are problems with these that repression – repressed aggression or sexual repression – rears its ugly head. So the two books are about all these four of Freud's ideas.

In this book, most of Section 1 (especially Articles 1-17) is largely about the aggressive drive and repressed aggression, though there are a few articles thrown in that don't quite fit into that category. And Section 3 – *'Being more reasonable in business'*, is related to the first Section in that it is largely about 'anger' that many of us experience – but in this case anger directed at businesses and corporations. (Inevitably perhaps, a book called *'Being more reasonable in business'* is actually more about businesses that are blatantly <u>unreasonable</u>.)

Section 2, a shorter section, called *'Hampshire journalism at the cutting edge'* is more 'general' in nature, consisting of a variety of insights I had on wide-ranging topics, during the 2010s, when I had retired from my businesses and was travelling (mainly) round Hampshire.

The title article is in the first Section (Article 3).

Note: *Some of the articles were written several years ago.*

* So – you may also be interested to read my sister book 'Mainly about conquering sexual repression' – get it at Amazon (or direct from my website).

If you look it up on Amazon, search for: Mainly about conquering sexual repression: Chris Burnell.

SECTION 1
Articles on Education and Social Studies

PART I
Social Studies

There is no common theme to the articles in this part, and therefore it would be difficult for me to write an introduction. So I think it's best to get right on into the fray – starting with an article about - of all things - Club/Dance music.

ARTICLE 1
Fun as Therapy

For a hundred years or more, psychologists have been trying to find ways to help people 'overcome their demons'. Various methods have been invented and tried. These include psychoanalysis, psychotherapy, encounter groups and transactional analysis. I'm not sure what degree of success is attributed to each of these.

Perhaps the above introductory paragraph isn't totally appropriate. People can overcome bad states in ways other than by getting involved with 'the caring professions' – a new job, an adventure, a holiday, new relationship, ending an old relationship, going shopping even, moving house – all sorts of things may help.

I would like to share with you a new way which I've found which has seemed to have had the effect of helping to overcome my 'bad states'.

You might laugh, as I am quite a bit out of the normal age-range for this – but what seems to do me so much good is listening to the latest Club/dance music – the music they play in the nightclubs these days.

I started getting interested in the latest pop music (again), a while ago, and bought quite a few CDs. By chance, one day I bought one of the Clubland series of CDs (they are Club music compilations) – I'm not really sure why – except that I did used to love nightclubs, when in my twenties.

Anyway, the day after playing this, peoples' reaction to me (e.g. the attitude of shop assistants to me in a store – simple things like that) – seemed to change – and for the better.

I connected the two things, and since then have added to my collection of this sort of music. And I'm convinced it really does make a big difference.

I know they say one man's meat is another man's poison, but it's the first thing I've done in a long time that's had this effect, and thinking about it, there does seem to be some logic to it. That is, that this kind of fast music does 'take you out of yourself' – it is hard not to forget about your various worries when this Club music is coming at you!

Maybe it will help other people too – who wouldn't normally think of buying CDs of this sort.

ARTICLE 2
The Need to Fail

I have discovered that we have a desperate <u>need</u> to fail. That's right, fail. Of course, we <u>want</u> to succeed, but our actual need is to fail.

But there is some good news. I have written elsewhere that according to psychoanalytic theory, we all, as children, needed a 'good enough mother' (but not a 'perfect' one). And also that we just <u>need</u> one or two 'fairly satisfactory' relationships or friendships (but not necessarily very satisfactory ones).

Well, my feeling is that there is an equivalence with these other things, and with our need to fail. In other words, we don't need to fail <u>totally</u>.

We can (and must try to) be a success in the things that matter in life. But to fulfil our need to fail, we must find a few things which we bungle. The good news is that these things we must find to be inferior or beaten at needn't be important things.

One of the secrets of a successful life is to allow oneself to fail at a few, unimportant things, to fulfil our <u>need</u> to fail. And this will leave us free to succeed in the big things.

But if we don't have that 'escape route' (failing at some unimportant things), we will find ourselves, driven by our need to fail, botching the big things.

There are a lot of people who won't like me saying what follows – but I'll go ahead anyway.

Professional sportsmen and women are driven by their desire to succeed in sport. I'm not arguing with that. But for most of the rest of us, it is a different story. Those of us who play, or have played, for example, football for an amateur Sunday league side – perhaps a works team – do not have the same outlook as the Harry Kanes of this world.

It is not the end of the world if we lose!

In fact, I believe that playing some sport where, quite frankly, our team (or us individually) isn't too successful, is one of the ideal ways we can satisfy our <u>need to fail</u>.

Looking back, I realise that when playing games like chess, or Scrabble, or anything like that, I unconsciously move into non – thinking mode.

It's not just that I 'switch off' every time I play a game. I genuinely don't have the kind of mind that would make me potentially good at these things. And I was a lousy computer programmer. I believe that I would never have been good at that, however many courses I might have attended, or books read. My brain just doesn't work that way.

For that reason it'd probably be a good idea for me to play these sorts of games more often. Losing – as I inevitably would (if my opponent knew what he/she was doing) – would be good for me.

There is an unfortunate trend in life. A higher and higher proportion of people are taking games and, particularly, sport far too seriously. Of course, as I've already implied, if you're a top professional footballer in the premiership earning £100,000 a week or even more, then it *is* serious. You'll have to find something else to fail at!

I've got to be careful here. I'm not saying you should not try to do your best. I believe that (most of the time) you should. If everyone participating in sport deliberately set out to lose, sport would, of course, lose its meaning.

All I'm saying is that it's important to find a few things which, even when you try your best at them, you are not all that good – and maybe some sport will help to fulfil that role for you. The mistake I have sometimes made in the past, is simply to avoid doing anything that I didn't feel I had a flair for.

What I'm saying is that, ideally, one should do a few things about which someone might say about us "Well he/she tries hard, but they're really not very good at it."

But hopefully, people will not say that about your main career. (When I was a failure at my work as a computer programmer, it was actually very stressful.)

ARTICLE 3

The Misfortune of a J K Rowling / Harry Potter Effect

1) One unfortunate result of the extreme popularity of the Harry Potter books is that a quite large percentage of people have become involved in witchcraft to a greater or lesser degree – especially women, but also some men. (For women especially) to 'know a few spells' is probably about as popular as it was for teenage boys and young men to try to learn the guitar during the main period of Rock music i.e. the 60s, 70s and 80s.

2) No-one is too clever to be a victim of witchcraft

Two extremely clever people who were victims of witchcraft were Shakespeare and Mozart – it killed both of them at a young age (youngish in the case of Shakespeare).

Shakespeare foolishly wrote his last major play about witchcraft – 'The Tempest'. He was never the same again. What he wrote after that was a pale shadow of what he had written previously, and he was dead within a few years of writing it.

In the case of Mozart I believe he was a bit involved with witchcraft in the last couple of years of his life, and composing 'The Magic Flute' (written as a result, I believe), killed him (he died just after the premiere).

About my evidence

I found this information about Mozart in a biography of him which was written a long time ago – about 100 years ago, I think. And I cannot now remember the title or author, unfortunately. I had joined a 'history book club' which specialised in history books and biographies of famous people that had been written many years previously – so the books were out of Copyright presumably – (because many small publishers baulk at the prospect of meeting and arranging contracts with living authors.). This biography of Mozart was one of the books I received from them.

As regards the comments about Shakespeare, I didn't read this in any book, but I did a bit of research on Shakespeare. I read 'The Tempest', so I knew it was 'largely about witchcraft'. And I soon found out that it was his last 'major play'. I discovered that he had in fact co-authored a few plays with other authors after writing 'The Tempest', but that these co-authored plays are by no means considered 'great works of art' in the same way that his famous plays are.

3) Sorry, I don't know much

To be honest, I don't know anything about 'how it's done'. I just know I had a relationship once with a young woman who told me she was a witch, and a few weeks later there were some "nasty effects". And 'attacks' by 'the witch' ultimately caused me to lose a very well paid job, and literally waste a dozen years of my life. (Basically, the 'attacks' by 'the witch' gave me symptoms of a nasty illness.)

ARTICLE 4
The Bad News and the Good News

If you're attacked by anyone (or by a group of people) – [and this is the 'bad news', by the way] – there is usually good news too.

The good news is that the chances are you are making a very positive impact on someone (or again, possibly a group of people).

So, whilst you may have to lick your wounds as a result of the attacks, there is probably something that you can pat yourself on the back, even congratulate yourself for – perhaps it is even something you don't know about.

This is because most attacks are due to jealousy. And this can only happen if you're making a very positive impression (or something equivalent) in some respect – and probably in a way that matters.

PS I don't just mean a violent (physical) attack – there are many forms.

ARTICLE 5

Man May (Basically) Be 'A Fighter' – But Against Whom - Or What?

[I believe it is good to keep 'in tune' with our distant ancestors. They were closer to nature, had their finger more on the pulse than we do – with our incredibly comfy lifestyles. If we can find some ways that are practical and reasonable to emulate their lifestyle in certain respects, I believe we will increase our 'life force' or energy level. In this case, other benefits may ensue too.]

I think we have to accept that men (probably less so most women), have a very powerful aggressive drive, which has to be 'accommodated' (shall we say) – otherwise some form of 'emotional sickness' sets in.

So, most men fight with their families – their parents, their children, their brothers, their friends (or more likely ex-friends), and their girlfriends or wives (or often ex-girlfriends or ex-wives.)

And the situation with people in authority can be even worse – they can often be 'bullying' (effectively) towards their subordinates, for instance.

Perhaps this has always been so.

OR HAS IT?

I haven't read the famous book 'A Brief History of Time', by Stephen Hawking, but presumably the earth's history goes back many millions of years.

Obviously, there has been virtually no evolution in the human race for at least the last 4000 years or so – (the ancient Greek men (for instance) seem to me to have been far more 'real men' – both intellectually and physically (brawn-wise), than most men these days, and I really think we have gone backwards since then in almost every way.

But what if we haven't really evolved much, since the days before not only reading and writing, but even speaking (as we know it), and therefore before much socialisation, and certainly before religions?

We would have been more of an 'island' than today.

Also, we say that we were hunters and fishermen. But perhaps fishing came before hunting – it would seem to be easier in some ways. And perhaps, again, we haven't really evolved much (in ways that really matter) since then.

To summarise – we haven't really evolved much since

We were all fishermen.

We hardly 'socialised' at all (as we know it).

We all lived by the sea.

And we have assumed that we all have a very powerful aggressive drive.

Where does this lead us?

Surely this is beginning to make sense?

It explains, for instance, almost everyone's love of the sea, doesn't it?

I am suggesting that life would have been very physical – men would probably have been very strong, compared to today. And also that men's fighting (i.e. 'accommodating' their aggressive drive), would have been against 'the elements' – the wind, rain, and – in particular, the forces of the sea – not really against people, so much.

So, my idea is that if we could imitate this scenario – this very physical fight against the elements, and the sea – then we may not need to fight in the ways we do at present, which are often so destructive.

The only way I can really think that we might be able to do this, is for us not only to take exercising seriously, but to make swimming an important part of our exercising. It may be that swimming, for this reason, is an even more valuable form of exercising than is already thought.

It would be an interesting experiment to see if people who do this show different, and preferable personality traits, on average.

Also – I can attest to the <u>very great</u> enjoyment and pleasure one can get from water sports (in my case sailing). I was involved in this as a teenager.

ARTICLE 6

Some Readers are so Widely Read – But is it an Asset?

It amazes me how many books some professors and people like that have read. Maybe 500, even 1000, in their specialist subjects. (With techniques like 'speed-reading', etc, I believe this is possible.)

But I really think that it may be more of a disadvantage rather than an asset. If your subject is 'sociology', for instance – I'm sure it's not great to have read 500 books on the subject, often with similar conclusions – (a lot of these tend to be exam-syllabus based, and at most universities, in a certain subject, a bit 'samey', shall we say.)

So surely it becomes rather like being on a train going along a railway line – and everyone has more or less the same line of thought – coming to roughly the same conclusions.

Contrast this with the Ancient Greeks. I read once, for instance, that Plato was known to be 'not widely read'. I wouldn't be at all surprised if that wasn't virtually the understatement of the century.

Probably the professor who found it out, and who wrote it (it was probably a professor), who had himself, I expect, read 400 - 500 books at least, in his speciality, was too embarrassed to admit that he had discovered that Plato had read perhaps no more than a dozen books in his life.

[I don't know for sure, but wouldn't be at all surprised.]

ARTICLE 7

About my Experiences with the Encounter Group Movement back in the 80S

I will just say a little about my experiences with the Encounter Group Movement roughly 35 years ago.

The Encounter group Movement was strong in the Eighties in particular. One of the many things people in the movement generally believed was that repressed aggression was rife – that there were a lot of 'aggression-phobic' people. Encounter groups – aiming to solve this problem – were considered quite trendy at this time.

There would usually be about a dozen people in the group – activities would be things like role play, but the main point of it was that everyone would be a lot more open about their feelings for other people in the group than is normal. For example, you might say what you found attractive or unattractive about someone else of the opposite sex. Or you might be encouraged to express any anger – sometimes this would be a full-blown argument – a blazing row even – two people would be shouting at each other (the air would be very blue!). The idea was that it was considered very good for you to get any anger out of your system.

As I said, they were thought very trendy – almost hippyish, but controversial too. Some church groups thought that they were more 'devilish' than had originally been thought of rock music when it first came out.

The people in this movement (who went to Encounter Groups) strongly believed that we had an 'aggressive-phobic' society, by which they meant that a high percentage of people would be very uncomfortable (would get very tense, even) in a situation where there were people expressing anger.

[I don't mean necessarily ranting and raving and banging the table, though it would include that; some people would be very uncomfortable about having someone express anger even in a normal voice.]

If you got into the Encounter Group scene, the chances were that one of your goals would not only be to get any anger out of your system, but generally to become a less 'aggression-phobic' person.

In fact, repressed aggression (being angry without realising it), or being aggression-phobic was thought by people in the movement to be responsible for quite a lot of major physical illnesses. It was said that heart disease and cancer could be caused by repressed aggression, for instance, as well as depression – and certainly suffering repressed aggression led to a reduced 'lifeforce'.

One of the most important things about the Encounter Group Movement is that people in it believed that the experience of gaining insight into the causes of any repressed anger or aggression (or other destructive emotions) could lead to being in a better state.

I was very interested in these theories at the time and found quite a few books with more or less this point of view in my local library – in fact I took one or two out to read. But recently I looked through the shelves of the library (the same one) and couldn't find a single book with this line. I think it is out of favour these days – actually it made me think of the situation in Communist countries where apparently everything was censored, and you could only find books in libraries pushing ideas that were in favour. It almost seemed like the same thing had happened here.

(But perhaps I shouldn't blame the libraries – there may well not even be hardly any books in print pushing this line anymore.)

But I am sure that finding safe ways of getting your anger out of your system (basically what the Encounter Group Movement was largely about) is enormously important.

And in fact, I believe that the Encounter Group Movement was more or less right, and we, in our culture today, who have turned our back on these ideas and gone in the opposite direction even, are wrong.

25

I will summarise some of the important points made in this article:-

- a) *repressed aggression is being angry without realising it – without being aware of the anger*
- b) *repressed aggression causes a reduced life-force*
- c) *becoming aware of what is making us angry leads to a better state (there is less repression)*
- d) *catharsis (getting anger out of our system) results in a considerably better state (as long as the way of doing it doesn't produce guilt)*

PS I am aware that I am not using the term 'repression' in quite the same way as, for instance, Freud did – but think that this approach (as outlined here) is quite workable.

ARTICLE 8
'Our Instincts'

They say that you're not well educated unless you've done a bit of studying about Freud. Well, Freud at first thought we had basically just one instinctual drive (<u>sex</u>), and later in his life added <u>aggression</u> to this. Adler, on the other hand, thought it was <u>power</u> that was the (just one) basic drive. From my own ideas, I like to think in terms of not one, not two, but six drives. (No doubt some could be 'subsumed' under others with the right arguments, so I'm not arguing that Freud or Adler were wrong, of course.)

The 6 instincts or 'drives' I have decided on are:-

Power

Sex

Aggression... with these first 3 in mind read Freud, Adler and their followers.

Performance (part a)... the need to 'give performances' (not necessarily in the traditional sense) – a lot of 'ordinary' things can be thought of as 'giving a performance' e.g. going to a nightclub (where we are very much 'on show').

Performance (part b)... The need to go to performances (given by others) [we need to be selective about this – not all types of performance will suit us].

Company... we need to be 'in company' some of the time.

Self-understanding... we need to attempt to understand ourselves, e.g. by reading literature or again, psychological books.

ARTICLE 9
How Boring is our Work?

I have been writing for quite a few years, and although I have only rarely sought publication as such, have made a habit, from time to time, of getting quite a few copies of 'my latest stuff' printed and giving these to people I met – in some cases friends, and at other times more-or-less strangers.

However, I suppose it's true that, for the first 2 or 3 years I was writing (especially), people tended not to like what I wrote much. I probably lost more friends than I gained, to be frank. But recently, those I've shown things to have been much more impressed, I've felt.

In the past, the booklets I've had printed have usually been A5 size. But when it came to some of my recent writing, the booklets I used for 'showing around' happened to be A4 size – simply because I used a different print shop than before.

And although I'm convinced that this latest writing is basically a lot more 'readable' than anything I've done before, I've met with an unusual reluctance for people actually to read it in the first place (in this latest case). Even when someone has taken a copy, I've noticed that 2 or 3 weeks later it's quite likely not been read.

And it has occurred to me that this may be because I used A4 size, rather than A5.

Thinking about it, A4 size paper is associated with documents and study material at both schools and colleges, and also at work. For example, A4 ring binders (used by school pupils and students) are much more common than A5 ones. Also, I've been looking through an office products catalogue recently – at binding machines in particular (usually used in offices), and they nearly all make books in A4 format.

Now, could this thing I've noticed – this greater reluctance to read my latest (A4) booklets – somehow be a sort of 'unconscious' thing? Could it point to the possibility that there are an awful lot of people actually quite angry about their experiences at school and/or work?

This article was written quite a few years ago – at that time I was mainly using short booklets – 20-25 pages usually.

ARTICLE 10
A Good Forgettery

Having 'a good forgettery' was how a teacher of mine, who was in her seventies then, described her bad memory.

Some of us have better memories than others, of course. I have a very bad memory for details.

What I would like to say is that I do not believe what is often taken for granted in psychotherapeutic circles – that all our past experiences are 'recorded' somewhere in our unconscious. The idea that we only have to find the right technique, and any experience from the past can be 'brought back' into our consciousness.

I believe we really do forget things, and once forgotten, they cannot be brought back.

Techniques such as hypnosis may well appear to 'bring back the past', but my belief is that it may just as likely be 'an imagined past', rather than the actual one, however competent the hypnotist appears to be.

To conclude, we really do have 'a good forgettery'.

ARTICLE 11
Become an Expert in Something

I believe one of the best ways of finding fulfilment is through learning – specialised learning – becoming an expert in something.

Most peoples 'interests' do not come into this category.

A lot of people are interested in gardening, for instance. But very few will really find fulfilment through gardening because very few are really expert at it.

You are only expert at something (this is my definition) if you know more about it than 99% of the population does.

An expert in gardening, for instance, wouldn't just need to know the names of most popular flowers and plants, and how to tend them successfully. He would have to have entire shelves in his bookcase full of books on gardening, and to have studied them assiduously.

Why? Because so many people know a great deal about gardening. To be in the top 1% as regards 'knowledge of gardening' one would really need to know an awful lot about it.

The same is true of all the very popular interests and sports e.g. football, cookery etc.

Anyone who chooses anything like this as their field in which to find fulfilment will need to have a very great capacity for acquiring knowledge, because the competition is so great.

Just imagine how 'word perfect' you'd need to be about football, for instance, to be in the top 1% as regards expertise about it. So many people spend such a lot of time thinking and reading about it (and presumably they learn a great deal).

Most of us, if we are to find fulfilment, must choose something that is much more of a minority interest.

ARTICLE 12
The Importance of the Two Week Cooling Off Period – and its Implications

We all know about the two week (or is it a 10 day) cooling off period for certain contracts e.g. for life insurance. However, I am talking about something different here.

Basically, I am talking about what is necessary after something (or somebody) has made us very angry.

I expect you've heard the advice – when you get angry about something count to 10 before you take any action.

My feeling is that more appropriate advice might often be to 'count to two weeks'.

I have written elsewhere about a type of anger that I believe normally requires a two week cooling off period. That was about a situation with just an acquaintance - obviously I wasn't living with her. (See my book *Mainly about conquering sexual repression*' – Article 8.)

Now I'll speculate a bit about the situation where a

couple <u>are</u> living together.

John Gray says a lot about this in his book *'Men are from Mars, Women are from Venus'* (and its sequels) and I recommend you read it.

It seems to me that if a couple are 'truly living' they could not help but fall out from time to time. The only way a couple could go through years and years of married life, for instance, and only extremely rarely have arguments or fall out, is if they repress a lot of their feelings as a matter of course.

I happen to believe that a lot of couples do indeed do this – see below.

But assume then, that the couple we are talking about don't repress too many of their own feelings. I would argue that they must have arguments, must fall out, from time to time. What happens then?

In the book referred to above (*'Men are from Mars, Women are from Venus'*), John Gray talks about the man 'going into his cave'.

Obviously Gray doesn't mean this literally – few people have caves to go to, do they?

I don't think he means it even semi-literally, in the sense of the husband going away for a few days, or something like that.

What he seems to mean is that the husband becomes more 'distant' in an emotional sense, and less communicative. While he is 'in his cave', it is not a good time for the wife to start intimate discussions, for example.

Gray suggests that the man goes into his cave during times of stress, and when he needs to 'sort things out'.

My feeling is, though, that if a husband and wife don't repress their feelings, the negative ones will occasionally be so strong that simply to go through an 'uncommunicative' spell of a few hours, or even two or three days, won't really be enough.

I would suggest that if a couple aren't going to resign themselves to a life of repressing their feelings about each other to a certain extent, actual separation – occasionally for a week or a fortnight perhaps – will sometimes be necessary.

What I'm saying is that in 90% of marriages (or couples living together), where it is very much the exception rather than the rule that one of the partners sometimes goes off alone for a while (i.e. at least a few days), <u>there</u>

<u>must be considerable repression of feelings</u>.

I don't really think that the 'norm' should be that a husband and wife sleep together in the same bed for virtually every night of their marriage – or even under the same roof.

Something has occurred to me that may be evidence that very many couples living together, either married or 'as if married' are indeed repressing huge amounts of feeling.

This is that so many of them seem to be happy with a life consisting, each day, of the following:-

Eight hours work (often soul destroying), eight hours sleep, and in the other third of the day, a few chores, an evening meal, and about five hours in front of the television.

It is my belief that anyone who can be happy with an existence like that <u>must</u> be repressing great amounts of feeling.

I suppose it's true to say I've been quite a moody person. But, probably because of this, I've 'developed' or 'discovered' 2 or 3 techniques for dealing with (overcoming) bad moods. The most useful one of them I've called 'generalised insight therapy'.

ARTICLE 13
Generalised Insight Therapy

It is well recognised, by writers such as Anthony Storr, that there is a relationship between creativity and aggression. And our language has phrases which point to this. For example, we talk about "getting our teeth into a problem".

Suppose something has caused great anger (either repressed or "at or near the surface"). The therapeutic method I have discovered is to use that experience to create "a bit of knowledge" - some idea or theory relating to the particular problem, which adds to our understanding of human nature in some way (or appears to have potential for doing so). It should be something that is not specific to yourself and the particular situation that caused the anger, but can be seen as having a relevance to a range of difficulties which many other people may face, and is able to help them i.e. it is a <u>generalised</u> bit of knowledge.

Another way of putting it is as follows:-

If you "use" (what you learn from) a nasty experience to tackle (and find a solution to) a wider, more generalised problem, there will be healing (from the effects of that unpleasant experience – e.g. any anger, whether it is repressed or not).

Here is an example of how I have used generalised insight therapy.

I did something which was very stupid and which, I believed, had hurt someone considerably (emotionally, not physically), as well as unnecessarily promising to make a part of my life miserable for the foreseeable future.

This made me furious with myself, and I was in grave danger of repressing this anger, which would have greatly affected my emotional health. In fact, for most of a day, it did just that – I felt "emotionally dead" and for example, when someone stopped their car by me, and asked me for directions, their reaction to me told me that I wasn't in a very good state.

This was a bad experience, and things probably wouldn't have improved, perhaps for a long time, if it hadn't been for my use of the new technique, which I had recently discovered.

This was as follows:-

After being "hit" by this, during the day I had two or

three drinks to relax me a bit, and then, at about 5.30, went down to a local pub (but not one I usually frequent), for two lagers (as it turned out).

There was a very friendly, vivacious and attractive barmaid, and a few customers (men) who were humorously bantering with her. Although I didn't join in, I appreciated the atmosphere. At the same time my mind was working overtime. And then afterwards, on the way home, I came up with the following "generalised insight".

If you are very angry with yourself about something, it is very important to be able to forgive yourself.

This should be done, if possible, by recognising that there were extenuating circumstances; and also by congratulating oneself on the positive things one has done in the recent (or even not so recent) past, hopefully with the conclusion that there have been more "positives" than "negatives". (If there are no extenuating circumstances, or if there aren't more positives than negatives, I'm not sure how to proceed, in fact.)

On the other hand, I feel that "forgiveness" of others when they have wronged you is often less healthy. Often when people 'decide' that they have forgiven someone for something, and act accordingly, especially if it is something serious, what they actually do is to repress their anger. This can cause great emotional damage.

When someone wrongs you badly, what is actually required is to sort of sum up the "positives" and "negatives" of that relationship. (This is a largely unconscious process, of course.) Obviously a serious "negative" has just entered into the equation, but provided the "balance" is more positive than negative, which will usually be the case in a good relationship or friendship, there is obviously no reason to finish it. And the thing that caused the anger should be forgotten (i.e. filed in the "no action taken" file – except, perhaps, to make the other person aware how he/she has made you feel.)

In the meantime, the negative emotion needs to be dissipated in as healthy and socially acceptable way as possible. For example, some people go for a long walk or dig the garden.

End of "generalised insight".

After this was composed, it was clear to me that the vexation surrounding the incident had gone.

This technique has been effective at eradicating quite a few of my bad moods.

[This next part is an addition to the original text. It is about another technique for overcoming bad moods. I doubt if it will be nearly so commonly used as the other one, but I think it's worth including.]

Defining the problem

Einstein, among others, was fond of saying that it was more difficult to "define a problem", than to then go ahead and solve it.

I have discovered that if you can use an experience which has made you very angry to, in some sense, define a problem, there will be complete relief from that anger. It is, I believe, an even more powerful technique than generalised insight therapy (because defining a problem is more difficult than solving it).

For various reasons, I do not want to give an example of its use. (I have only used it once and it is not appropriate to describe that.)

Guilt

Guilt and anger at yourself are the same thing. They are equivalent.

Therefore, generalised insight therapy (which fights against anger), is very appropriate to be used to combat guilt.

For example, a recent "generalised insight" relating to something I felt very guilty about, was simply:-

"It's okay to make mistakes." (Sometimes – as on this occasion – I had found it difficult to forgive myself when I made mistakes.)

Incompetence

Incompetence is sometimes a sin (wrong). In fact, it can be one of the worst.

When it is a sin, it is appropriate to feel guilty about it. And therefore, generalised insight therapy can be used to deal with this too.

You may be surprised to hear me say that incompetence is <u>sometimes</u> a sin. Surely it either is or isn't.

I believe this is not so. It is as if, at certain times in our life, we choose what we are going to be good at, and also what to be bad at.

For example, one of the "choices" I have made is to be bad at D.I.Y. That decision is helped by a complete lack of aptitude. And I know that I would have been hopeless as an engineer. Anything connected with "engineering" goes right over my head.

So anyway, we select the things to be bad at, and good at. Hopefully we decide to be good at what we have an aptitude for, and likewise what to be bad at by noting a lack of ability. (But I suppose that doesn't always follow.)

Now, if we are incompetent at what we have chosen to be good at, that is a sin.

But if we make mistakes relating to things we have "decided" to be bad at, that is not a sin.

Therefore, I can laugh at my incompetent attempts at D.I.Y. because they are not sins. But I can get very upset at incompetence at what I'm supposed to be good at.

Incidentally, I'm sure we can't "choose" to be a bad parent, or certain other things; e.g. not to be safety conscious. It's just not allowed.

ARTICLE 14

When You're Looking for a Job, Think of the Perks

In my case, because I did well in my A-levels, I went to Oxford; later, because I had a maths degree I went into computing.

At Oxford while I was there, there was about a 5:1 ratio of men to women. There was also what they called a "town and gown split" - people from the university rarely mixed with everyone else in Oxford. The upshot of it was that it was actually quite difficult for male students there to find girlfriends – many male students didn't have a girlfriend the whole time they were there, even though, in some respects they were among the most eligible young men in the country – and quite a lot from very rich families too (a high percentage had been to a public school).

Again, when I was a software engineer, there were far more men than women. It wasn't quite as bad as for mechanical or electronic engineers – in that there were hardly any women – but still the ratio wasn't much different from at Oxford.

That was me.

Now I think of the landlady, Lee, at my local until recently. Her son became a hairdresser (he is about the same age as me.) That is a profession that is looked down on, to some extent, considered low status – or it used to be anyway. In fact, Lee's husband, who had been an RAF pilot, was apparently extremely upset when the son made this decision.

But Lee told me that this son had "a ridiculous number" of girlfriends – what she was saying made me quite envious in a way. The point was he had an ideal job, really, for chatting up women. Basically, he had probably at least a dozen women in his chair each day for half an hour or so each, who were really a captive audience. No wonder he scored.

So that is going from one extreme to the other, jobwise, in that respect.

And I sometimes wonder if I was so clever to go to Oxford, for that reason alone.

I think if I had my time again, that 5:1 ratio would have put me off quite a bit. (It's changed now, at Oxford, by the way – most colleges accept both sexes.) Likewise with the career choice.

And come to think of it, surely for a normal heterosexual

person, having a job where you very frequently come into contact with a lot of attractive people of the opposite sex is a big plus point. It is very common for certain things to be valued in financial terms apart from the wages; e.g. you will be told that that company car is "worth" £5000 a year or whatever (and these days taxed heavily on that basis too).

But I'd put a high value on, as I said, having a job where you frequently come into contact with people you find attractive - if you're single, anyway.

The moral of this is – if you're lucky in this respect and have been offered a job with £2000 a year more or something, think twice if it means a deterioration from the above-mentioned point of view. Or, if you're thinking of a career change, don't just consider the money angle!

ARTICLE 15
Choose Hobbies that are "Unisex"

This is a similar point, really, to what I said about your career (article 14).

You are presumably going to choose a couple of interests to make your major hobbies, and I think it makes real sense to choose ones that appeal to both sexes.

Therefore, if you are a man, don't make chess your hobby (for some reason hardly any women are interested in that), but I would recommend something like photography or sailing.

Both men and women enjoy these greatly and that person you meet will probably be really pleased if they find one (or both) of them are ones that they can become interested in too.

Of course, if you can afford your own boat (and I'm not talking about a 30 foot yacht – just a sailing dinghy even, perhaps), and join a sailing club on the coast, a lot of people would jump at the chance of going with you – for this reason I'd recommend getting a boat that can be sailed by 2 or 3 people, not one that is very much a one person effort. (And for this same reason, I'd recommend "proper" sailing, rather than windsurfing.)

ARTICLE 16

The Healing Power of (Live) Music

Written in about 2012

I suppose the story starts about 4 years ago. I thought that as Shakespeare was regarded as easily our greatest writer, it was foolish not to make some attempt to find out what he had said – he surely would have put some of his secrets of "living" into his writing. However, I hadn't been much good at English literature at school, and I didn't feel like suddenly becoming a literature student and seriously studying a lot of his plays.

So, I did the next best thing: As I suspected, in the "*Oxford Dictionary of Quotations*" there were a lot of "quotations" by Shakespeare (actually mostly extracts from his plays) – there were many more pages devoted to Shakespeare than for any other person. I thought that even just reading these out of context (of the rest of the play) could well produce dividends. So I spent half an hour a day for about a week reading through these, in the library.

One of the main things, I thought, was that Shakespeare seemed to think that music had a magical property – that it could really have a "good effect" on us. There were quite a few quotations where music, or something related to music, was mentioned (just about always in a positive way) – and I remember getting that distinct impression.

There may have been other reasons as well, but about this time I started to buy quite a few music CDs, mostly from the top 100 album chart. I was regularly buying the "Now That's What I Call Music" compilation CD and would buy the CD by an artist if I liked their track on this. Over a few months I built up a bit of a collection.

Now, a lot of people will say, quite rightly, I suppose, that you don't need Shakespeare to tell you that music is "good". That it is quite self-evident. And most people work it out for themselves. I accept all that of course. It's just that in my case, it was reading those Shakespeare comments about music that was the catalyst – if you want to put it like that. And at that time I did change my "behaviour pattern" - from buying CDs just occasionally, to getting them very regularly, perhaps 2 or 3 a week, for quite a few months. And I was playing them for 2 or 3 hours a day, hoping for this "magic effect" to hit me.

But to be honest I was a bit disappointed. They didn't seem to help lift a depression which was attacking me a bit. In fact, after a while I bought CDs more occasionally again.

[Changing the subject]

My mother owns a caravan in Selsea, Sussex, and about 3 times a year I would go with her there for 4 or 5 days – my brother would drive us as I don't have a car (neither does my mother).

The caravan is on a very large site (Bunn Leisure), which is divided into 3 sections, and each section has club facilities – a large clubhouse and bar, for instance. Every weekend evening (and every night during the high season) they have entertainment at these clubhouses. This is very often a band. In fact, at the largest of the three clubhouses they have entertainment every night for most of the season.

Most evenings when we were down there, we would go into the bar and sometimes the clubhouse for a drink, but we usually didn't see much of the band because my mother goes back to the caravan about 9 to have her usual early night (also she usually found the band's music a bit loud for her taste). And for a long time I didn't feel like continuing drinking alone (on these occasions), so I went back to the caravan then too.

But in April 2009, when we went for the first time of the year, for 2 evenings running – a Saturday and a Sunday – I did stay to watch the bands – their complete performance.

The first was a group which had been famous when I was a youth, back in the early 70s – Mungo Jerry. Mungo Jerry himself, the band's singer, looked much younger than he must in fact be – his most famous hit, "*In the summertime*", came out in 1970, I think. I remembered quite a few of their songs and had a really enjoyable evening. (There was a support group of 2 girl singers called *Honey,* who were also very good – they sang a lot of hits of the last 15 years or so.)

Then on the Sunday, having enjoyed the previous evening so much, I went to the other clubhouse (the Embassy) where they had another group. It was called *Now 90s* – obviously it played hits from the 90s. Again, a very enjoyable evening.

But the best part was to come. After this weekend, I found that a stress-related ailment I had been suffering from had dramatically improved.

Of course, I thought it must have been because I had seen those 3 groups over the weekend. However, we had to go home on Monday. But I resolved to come back down to the caravan as often as possible over the next few months and see as much "live" music as I could.

It was fortunate that the nature of my work meant that I could do it wherever I pleased; and my mother agreed that I could use the caravan every other week (for 4 or 5 days) during May and June anyway.

In one of the clubhouses (though not the nearest one to our caravan – it involved a short bus journey) – they had live musical entertainment practically every night of the week, so I was confident that I could devote a lot of time to that and see if that initial beneficial effect was a coincidence or not. The stress-related ailment had greatly improved, but wasn't <u>completely</u> better. I wanted to see if seeing lots of live music would get it completely better.

Anyway, I continued going to Selsea for 4 or 5 days every 2 or 3 weeks throughout the season, and also when I was back in Andover I saw quite a bit of other entertainment, mainly at *"The Lights"* in Andover and *"The Anvil"* in Basingstoke (and also in pubs). And my stress-related ailment continued to improve.

This article is mainly about the "healing effect" of listening to live music. I am talking about "emotional healing" here of course, or to put it another way "healing from stress-related ailments".

Now, when we think of what we can see or hear at theatres / entertainment complexes / concert halls it seems to me there are 3 "biggies" - we can watch a play, we can listen to music, or we can see a comedian (and of course some plays are comedies and there is even musical comedy).

And I've said how our greatest thinker, Shakespeare,

praised music to the skies and wrote a lot about the "good effect" music can have on us. (And I've given one example of the "healing effect" of music in my own life.)

But when we come to the other 2 "biggies" - watching a play or seeing a comedian, although Shakespeare didn't directly "praise those things to the skies" in his writing, as he did with music, he was actually <u>intimately involved</u> with both of them. That is, he wrote plays (some of which were comedies), he was even fond of having characters who were comedians (e.g. Feste in Twelfth Night) and he even put "bits of comedy" in his more serious plays (e.g. King Henry IV part 1). And he was an actor too.

So you could say his being intimately involved with these two other "biggies" is (indirectly) even greater praise than the way he praised music (directly) in his writing.

So (after thinking these things through) I then had another hypothesis to test; namely, that watching plays, or seeing comedians, may have just as great "emotional healing power" as listening to music.

[And incidentally, just as I believe seeing bands play "live" has greater "healing power" than listening to CDs, I was quite expecting to find that watching a play has greater power than watching television and seeing a comedian live has much more power than looking at a DVD of that comedian.]

And so, my next task was to start seeing plays and comedy performances (as well as continuing to see the live music).

So, I began seeing plays – at *Chichester Festival Theatre* when I was staying at Selsea, and usually at the *Salisbury Playhouse* when back in Andover (and also saw comedy performances). And I was pleased to discover that I felt so much better after I had done so – as far as I was concerned my hypothesis that "emotional healing" would also result from seeing plays and watching comedy has been proved true.

ARTICLE 17

Bunn Leisure Caravan Site as a Kind of "Model" - Enjoying "Live" Entertainment Rather Than TV

Note: This article was written several years ago – before Bunn Leisure was taken over by another company that seems to think only of the profit motive – and now the entertainment it provides is not nearly so good.

PART 1 – My feelings about TV

The TV licence people certainly assume that everyone watches TV (a lot of the time, actually) otherwise they wouldn't practically accuse you of being a criminal whilst you have no licence (for a long time I didn't watch TV at all).

But I personally think it's an absolute waste of a life to watch as much TV as most people do. It's certainly "second-hand living" as far as I'm concerned.

I have an idea of how it needn't be the case that nearly everyone spends 4 or 5 hours virtually every evening watching TV. The idea is to use what they do at Bunn Leisure caravan site as a kind of "model".

PART 2 – Bunn Leisure as a kind of "model"

Bunn Leisure in Selsea, West Sussex, is actually 3 caravan sites in one, and each has its own clubhouse where plenty of entertainment is put on. The biggest clubhouse is the Embassy, which mainly serves the largest of the 3 caravan sites – West Sands.

The 3 sites together contain, I believe, about 5000 caravans, making Bunn Leisure the largest caravan site in Europe. The site fee to have your caravan there is about £3000 a year, so you can see it's a big business, certainly.

Fortunately, they are generous with their money when it comes to providing entertainment – though to be honest I haven't got a clue what <u>percentage</u> of that £3000 site fee is spent on it.

The Embassy has entertainment on every evening during the season from April to October. The other two clubhouses (JBs and Viking) only have entertainment on Friday and Saturday nights except during school holidays, when they have it every night of the week.

The entertainment goes on 'til nearly 11.30 anyway, and at weekends (and every night during the school holidays,

59

when the site is most busy) there is something on 'til 2am.

Our caravan is not on the biggest of the 3 sites, but fortunately (as I have no car) they run a free bus service every half hour between the 3 sites, so I can easily get to and from the Embassy.

Before I go on to talk in detail about the entertainment Bunn Leisure put on, let's compare this situation with what we find in my home town – Andover.

Andover must have about 20,000 households (compared with 5000 caravans at Bunn Leisure). And the fact that these 4 times as many people are offered live music entertainment that is (in quantity anyway) very much poorer, I think is appalling.

For 3 or 4 years we have had The Lights which is a 250-seat theatre used mainly for music entertainment (and sometimes comedians). It is excellent as far as it goes, though doesn't really attract many young people (and hardly any children). There are usually a couple of events a week during the "seasons", usually on Friday and Saturday. They often have quite well-known bands or singers (though usually well-known mainly from their music of 20 or 30 years ago). Not all of what they have on appeals to me, however. I might fancy one event a week on average, I would say. Most performances are priced at between £12 and £18 per ticket.

Apart from that, there are really just the pubs (and until 4 years ago that's <u>all</u> we had). About 3 or 4 of the pubs in Andover put on bands sometimes. Again, it is nearly always Friday or Saturday.

The upshot is that I rarely go out more than 2 evenings a week – and as far as I can see there is not much opportunity to. I think what <u>is</u> on offer during most of the week – a few pubs with jukeboxes, but mainly pubs with all their bars surrounded with TV screens, nearly always with football on – I think is terrible. It doesn't appeal to me at all. Surely a place with 70 000 people could do much better than this.

Contrast this with what I can do when in Selsea (I'm there usually one week in every 3 between April and October). I go out to see live music entertainment <u>every night</u> – 'til 11.30 on weekdays and 2 am on Friday and Saturday – heaven by comparison.

I will now talk in detail about the entertainment that Bunn Leisure put on.

On Fridays and Saturdays, in all 3 clubhouses, they usually have 'outside' bands, usually of a very good standard, and sometimes very well known. Some of the bands and singers they've had on in the last year, for instance, are The Jive Aces, Showaddywaddy, Ben Mills (an X-Factor finalist), Go West, Katrina, Billy Ocean, Chesney Hawkes, Gareth Gates, Alvin Stardust.

Generally they do two 45 minute sets. And between these, one of Bunn Leisure's 'resident' singers comes on for half an hour or so. And then, assuming it is a Friday or Saturday (or school holidays) another 'resident' singer will perform, in a smaller venue, between 12 and 2am.

So, as far as the main Friday and Saturday night entertainment goes, it is rather similar to what The Lights offers, except everyone is sat round tables drinking, it has a 'clubhouse' format (whereas The Lights is like a theatre).

But it's these 'resident' singers that really make Bunn Leisure different. For they not only perform between the sets of the major bands on a Friday and Saturday, but all the rest of the week too.

It's not only singers actually – they have dancers too; and they put on shows, or 'productions', usually two a night, from Sunday to Thursday.

Just to give you some idea, a few of these productions are 'Are you ready to rock?', 'Get ready for the weekend', 'Steps Club 7', 'Solid Soul', 'Destination USA', Cool Britannia, Revolution (a Beatles tribute), Divalicious (all girls), Icon – George Michael, Icon – Kylie, Icon – Robbie Williams.

This gives you some idea that there are rather a lot of these 'productions', and some of the names give an idea of the type of music. In a typical production, there might be two singers, and perhaps 4 or 5 dancers (girls). They often wear quite sexy costumes, especially the dancers.

Again, just as on Fridays and Saturdays, between the 2 (45 minute) 'productions' there will be one of their singers singing on their own for half an hour or so. So altogether the total entertainment is for about 2 hours – usually from 9 to 11.15.

I believe they have about 7 singers and roughly the same number of dancers. Also, a couple of the singers do most of the compering. (They also employ quite a few more 'minor' entertainment staff called Teamstars – for example, they nearly always have two of these dancing on the dancefloor, and they also look after the kids – with a 45 minute spot for them in the early evening (after that a lot of the kids go off to a separate room where they are entertained, again by Teamstars).

But most of the entertainment, for the adults anyway, is provided by about 15 people. And they do so for the whole week. And when the site is at its busiest the entertainment goes on 'til 2am (between midnight and 2am they usually have one of their singers performing, though occasionally two.)

Admittedly the music provided by these resident

entertainers is only really 'half live' – it is singers singing to backing tracks – they don't have a full band backing them. I suppose they would need to roughly double the number of entertainment staff to do that – have about a dozen musicians too.

But that is my 'model' for what I believe could (and should) happen in a 'non-holiday' place like my home town, so that all of us would have a much better alternative to watching TV for 4 or 5 hours every evening.

....

Music and drama have been very significant for us for at least 3,000 years – since, for instance, the time of Sophocles. But it is not now so significant, apparently, that we can find (and pay for) 15 people who can sing, dance, and provide 'live' entertainment when we want it (as Bunn Leisure do), in a town like Andover, with a population of 70 000.

Not only is this sort of thing not available in my home town, or in other similar places throughout the country, or indeed, in hardly any much larger places in the country – but we are making even further cuts in this direction. (The Arts Council funding is being reduced by 30%.) The mind boggles at the stupidity of it all!

....

As far as it goes, I have only praise for The Lights in Andover, which is run by Hampshire County Council. But I would be more ambitious than that. The kind of set-up I have in mind is suggested by thinking of Bunn Leisure as a kind of 'model', as I said.

Firstly, premises would be needed. But I think there is no reason why a couple of large warehouse spaces in the town (for instance, Andover, but actually, any average-size provincial town) couldn't be converted and fitted out. So it needn't cost a fortune from that angle.

So – just as with Bunn Leisure, about 15 singers and dancers could be employed who could rehearse and put on 'productions' throughout the week.

The idea is that the average family (with an average income) could go out several times a week and be entertained (maybe as much as 5 or 6 or even 7 times a week), so just as with Bunn Leisure, an entrance fee wouldn't be charged (at least when the 'resident' performers were on, probably 5 evenings a week – when 'outside' bands were booked probably a charge could be made).

Not only that, but drinks would be much cheaper too (than pubs). I would say charge about as much as Wetherspoons do for beer, maybe. But soft drinks should be available at supermarket prices (e.g. a can of coke can be obtained from supermarkets for about 50p [if bought in packs of 6]). This would mean that refreshments could be provided, especially for the children (or teetotal adults) <u>very</u> cheaply. The idea would be that a whole family could go out, say, 5 times a week (if they wished) for about £60 (allowing £12 per evening for refreshments). This cost would be affordable even for low-income families, provided they weren't up to their eyes in debt to banks, building societies and credit card companies. (And even more so, it would be affordable to couples or single persons.)

It would therefore be a very viable (and in my view, far superior) alternative to watching TV for 4 or 5 hours of an evening, virtually every night.

PS I think a group of 15 or so singers and dancers would only be able to rehearse for about a week of performances and wouldn't really be able to change their repertoire more often than about every 4 months (I think that's roughly what Bunn Leisure do). But there might be a dozen reasonably-sized towns in a typical region, so the dozen 'companies' could move from town to town, on a kind of rota, so that the acts seen in any one town would be different each week.

PPS This needn't be <u>that</u> expensive, I don't feel. If the average salary for the singers and dancers was £50,000, that would be a total of £750,000 for our hypothetical town (say £1 million, because it costs more to employ people than just their wages). Then you would need perhaps a couple of sound engineers, a couple of lighting persons, a choreographer, a voice coach maybe – i.e. a few support staff. Hopefully there would be some profit in the drinks, which would pay for the bar staff. The premises would cost too... perhaps if we estimated about £2 million as an annual cost of everything – of running this thing in a town like Andover, we wouldn't be far out.

And incidentally, there are a very large number of very talented singers, musicians and dancers who are 'unemployed' (at least, who haven't got a full-time job in music), and I feel it would be no trouble at all to recruit suitable performers.

PART II
Education

ARTICLE 18
On Education (1)

Note: Some of the comments in this article are a bit 'tongue in cheek', I suppose – for instance I don't think I'm seriously suggesting that we don't study history.

When you think about it, secondary education has been based for years on studying about 8 to 10 subjects at a 'moderate' level (GCSE) and usually three subjects at advanced level, if the pupil stays on for the 6th form.

In particular, the 8-10 subjects at GCSE level were, for many years, virtually the same for everyone, with very little difference between syllabuses.

I do not think there is anything wrong with that as such. It's just that for ages schools have been teaching the <u>wrong things.</u>

It is a standing joke that whenever a child comes home

from school and their mother or father asks them what they have been doing at school today, the child always replies, "oh nothing much".

I think it has always been thought that that was because secondary school years were sort of 'uncommunicative' years.

But what if, when a child says, "nothing much", he or she actually means more or less that – or rather, "nothing much that is relevant to me" – nothing much that I can talk about to you, or my friends, or anyone.

If you listen to school children talking amongst themselves, how often do you hear them talking about what they have learnt during their lessons at school?

Hardly ever, I'd say.

But there is no reason why this should be so. I think it ought to be possible to make lessons interesting enough so that pupils want to and do talk about what they have learnt at school amongst themselves.

For example, for over 100 years I'm sure, probably quite a significant part of the English curriculum has been poetry. I suppose some people are interested in this, but almost certainly very few.

Consider this. As a regular pub goer, it is impossible to avoid going to karaoke sometimes – though I haven't sung at them. But I often look at the screen, and I am always amazed at how wonderful the lyrics are to many of the songs. (I am not exaggerating at all. I very often think the lyrics are almost incredible.)

Yet I never felt that about the poetry we were told to read at school.

So why not, just as an instance, instead of studying the poetry the latest Poet Laureate has written, that practically no one except the "elite" can make head nor tail of – why not instead study (or analyse, or whatever you do), the lyrics of the latest pop tunes?

I'm sure that is what kids would be delighted to do, and they would talk about what they learnt when they socialised together too.

And isn't that what education is really for?

Surely this is where democracy is really valuable. Educationists shouldn't be saying to the kids "this is what you will learn", but "what would you really like to learn about?" - and when they find out, they should try to teach them that.

Okay, in this instance it may mean retiring off a few English teachers, who are only interested in John Betjeman and his ilk – and haven't got a clue what's in the top 40 – but that's life.

What I'm saying is that it really wouldn't matter if everyone <u>did</u> learn more or less the same things, as long as they were considered <u>relevant</u>, and which they really wanted to learn.

It was this sort of reasoning (but which I hadn't conceptualised at the time), that made me very interested in the Radical school movement while I was a student. Schools like Summer Hill – does it still exist? Apparently, they just told the kids, "Oh go and do what you like today" – and that happened every day. (And sometimes some of the kids chose to read a few books!)

It sounds a joke, but I wouldn't be surprised if some of them did quite well in the end.

I'm not recommending anything that radical for the English state school system, by the way. But examining things and the sort of movement towards 'relevance' – that I have exemplified by suggesting studying the lyrics of pop tunes, rather than traditional poetry.

Maybe I will say a little bit more.

It is one of the 'fundamentals' of British law that, when it comes to being charged, prosecuted or whatever, ignorance (of the law), is apparently no defence. Therefore, I think it absolutely crazy that (certainly until recently – I'm not sure what the situation is now) nothing about the law is usually taught in schools. I don't think we all need to know much about criminal law, contract law or whatever. But, for instance, when you go to the Citizen's Advice Bureau, the people you see are usually just ordinary people, usually with other jobs, I believe. I shouldn't think their training is that extensive (time wise). Surely it would be a good idea for virtually everyone to learn more or less what they learn – it probably wouldn't be the equivalent of more than one or two GCSE's.

Certainly, I think we should all be reasonably knowledgeable about, for instance, the Consumer Credit Act and the Sale of Goods Act. Surely we need to know about things like that, just to go shopping?

What we should not learn.

It's a nice idea that everyone should be able to speak French, but it just doesn't work, does it? It must just be too bloody hard once you are over 5 or something.

I was in the "A" stream in a grammar school, and had about 5 French lessons a week, for 5 years. And at the end of it, hardly anyone could speak French at all fluently, or understand a real French person speaking

French unless they slowed down to about a fifth of the normal speed.

I know everyone goes abroad these days (except me). But (isn't it true?), everyone goes to hotels where all the staff – even the cleaners probably – speak English.

We have never really been very well liked by the French. And those few who decide to be 'cultured' and drive round the villages of France and have a few bevies in the local with the regulars, probably, if the truth be known, aren't usually very welcome. (Especially if they try out their pidgin French.)

And history as well.

In pubs and cafés, I never hear anyone talking about the younger Pitt, or even Admiral Nelson, except possibly as part of a 1 liner – that goes over most peoples' heads.

And is it worth it just for that? I know it's nice to think that our great men and women from a few centuries ago will never be forgotten, but anyway some of them weren't all that nice.

The Victorians, for instance: a lot of them had religious views that were so extreme, they wouldn't be out of place in some of those fundamentalist sects you read about these days.

For those who are so keen that the past shouldn't be forgotten, there is some hope.

I think it likely that a few figures from the past may be 'resurrected' as being the 'acknowledged master' in a certain area of life, and studied because of that, for ages.

For example, I read that Julius Caesar and others of the period were expert orators, and generally superb at 'giving a performance' – maybe people can dig up his (their) secrets in that field.

There is an expression in computing called 'garbage in – garbage out'. It means that if you feed nonsensical information into a computer you can't expect to get anything but rubbish out of it.

Maybe in education, we should think 'something in – something else out'.

That is, if we learn something, we should realise that something else (we previously learnt) might well be forgotten.

I read once that Einstein deliberately didn't remember his own telephone number – he always looked it up in the telephone directory – surely it must have been on that principle!

So – we should make sure that what we learn is of considerable value to us.

ARTICLE 19
On Education (2)

One Aspect Of Authoritarianism, In Our Schools – We Get Used To It At A Young Age!

I spent 13 years at school, and during that time (apart from the first two years*), in virtually all the lessons, the teacher was talking for most of the time. (Except that the teacher might ask quite a few questions – and if you knew the answer you were expected to raise your hand, and if you were chosen by the teacher you could (briefly) give your answer to the question.)

Talk about giving all the power to the Executive!

I don't know if the situation has changed much in the time since I was at school, or not. But I was planning to go to teachers training college much more recently and spent several days in a comprehensive school as a 'trial' situation – to see if I might like being a teacher – and I have to say that at that time, nothing much had changed.

* In the first two years I was at school, I remember

the teacher spent a great deal of time listening to the children read.

ARTICLE 20
On Education (3)

Now I will say a little about higher education – I'll say why I think there's a lot wrong with that.

When I was in my final year at university, most students worried more about the looming final exams than the employment situation. But, of course, the time when you would be going for interviews was the same time effectively that you might be preparing for exams – which really took the whole of the last two terms (out of 3) of the final year.

But we were advised not to apply for more than 3 or 4 jobs. We were told it was almost certain you would get a couple of offers if you applied for the 3 or 4, so it was pointless 'spreading your net too wide' - it would only leave you too many choices - and you might not get such a good degree. (This was Oxford, by the way – the situation probably wasn't quite so rosy at most other universities.)

Also, for most jobs it didn't matter what degree you had done. Most people who went in for accountancy, for instance, would have done nothing like that at university. It was only really for engineering, and of course medicine, that you had to have done the specialised subjects.

Also, of course, you got a reasonable grant, and no-one I knew did any paid work during term time – it would have been thought ridiculous.

How things have changed, haven't they?

I haven't had much connection with recent graduates these last few years, but from what I have, it seems to me that:-

a) If you get a poor degree, you're on the scrap heap no matter what subject it is.

b) If you do 'the wrong degree' (i.e. a non- vocational one) you are on the scrap heap even if you get a first. (I know someone who recently got a first in anthropology from a very reputable university – and she could do no better than work effectively as a care assistant.)

Anything like anthropology or history seems to be a waste of time these days.

Not only that, but I believe the finances are such that you not only have to pay large amounts back after you graduate, but you are also expected to take paid work for 12-15 hours a week while a student to make ends meet too (even during term time).

All this is totally crazy.

Apparently, the idea is that 50% of teenagers go to university. I think this is pretty ridiculous. A lot of people just haven't got the aptitude for that amount of studying. And what's the point anyway, if you're only going to get quite a menial job, probably near the minimum wage, at the end of it?

(When I was that age people wouldn't do some jobs that you now apparently need a degree for, if they had a couple of O-Levels!)

I'll now talk about teaching at universities (and research).

It seems to be universal all over the world that academics spend some of their time (maybe half) doing research, and the rest of their time teaching.

Yet I don't see the logic in this at all. They seem to be completely unrelated jobs – nothing in common really. It's like – I don't know – saying that all professional footballers also have to be professional mathematicians.

Many of these academics also write books. I think there's no question that if someone is trying to do research and teaching, and at the same time is writing a book – then he or she is grossly overworked.

SECTION 2
HAMPSHIRE JOURNALISM AT THE CUTTING EDGE

(This was (mostly) written in 2017.)

Receptionist Joke 1

These days when you see new houses for sale – ordinary ones about £300,000 (maybe). Then, a few at £450,000 - £550,000……. And it says (regarding the latter) – 'Architect designed'.

So who designs the 'ordinary' £300,000 ones? Is it the flippin receptionist?

Receptionist Joke 2

It seems the receptionists run all the hotels these days. They certainly make all the major decisions. Like:

Are we fully booked or not? If not – how much to charge? It can be anything from £30 to £120 – for the 'less expensive' ones (the same hotel can go from one extreme to the other from one week to the next). (This week's figure is seemingly chosen at random, or perhaps what mood she is in – or come to that, whether she likes you or not.)

And when the manager pops in at 11, she tells him "It's alright, I've got everything in hand."

Manager Joke 1

It has never been like this before. 30 years ago, managers did do some work, but never the flipping typing. These days they always do – it takes up 80% of their time (and it would have taken a typist about 20 minutes!).

* *I'm talking mainly about emails, of course.*

About Dentists

I will talk about two things related to them.

First – X-rays

For my first 40 years (approximately) I had a dentist who virtually never gave me X-rays (I can't even remember one time, actually).

But since then (after my previous dentist closed down) I have had a dentist who insists on giving me X-rays almost every year. I have complained several times that I don't like having X-rays, but they take no notice. And I have read that the X-ray guns that they use are lethal.

There is certainly very well documented evidence that people who have quite a few X-rays given by their dentist are several (perhaps many) times more likely to develop mouth cancer than those who don't.

So why on earth do dentists apparently have to give people quite a lot of X-rays (over years, of course) these days, when they managed quite well without them when I was young. To me this seems a mark of <u>total</u> incompetence.

The second thing - "braces"

A fairly high proportion of people will have repetitive, soul destroying jobs as adults, which will leave them – soul destroyed.

Therefore for these people, their childhood (and possibly retirement if they live that long), will be the best years of their lives. So anyone who inflicts damage on them during these "purple years" is doubly guilty.

But think of dentists putting braces on the teeth of so many children during their adolescent years, decimating their attractiveness. It is absolutely disgusting, in my opinion.

There Is One Thing (Anyway) In Christianity That I DO Agree With

(St Paul basically said – 'Give up childish things.')

But – flipping heck – have you heard even the top people's humour – and the films they see? Literally 'Why did the chicken cross the road?' – the exact same jokes that 5 year olds used to tell – then they (the top people) laugh like mad. And their favourite films are children's films too. And if a 20 something bloke is chatting up a woman he might say: "What is your favourite Disney actor." (Yes, I've heard that uttered – it's not imagination.)

Another Crazy Thing

People did use to tell jokes sometimes (quite often actually). Some quite good ones too. And there was a skill to it. You would admire someone who told jokes well. These days it appears to have become a forgotten skill. Jokes are still sometimes 'shared' – but usually this just means someone shows someone else a joke (as a text message) on their mobile phone. This is just a caricature. You might just as well take a joke book along to the pub and say "Turn to page 111, there's a good joke there!"

On Headlines (in the papers)

(That you would never have got 30 years ago.)

e.g. 'Emily Thornberry's chubby little fingers clawed in and out'   (Daily Mail)

Emily Thornberry is Shadow Foreign Secretary and is noted for being an exceptionally good public speaker. Now, it has always been the case that certain politicians have been hated by sections of the press, but so far as I can recall the attacks did not seem to be so puerile and obnoxious as this.

Another SAMPLE bit of writing

On The NHS

The NHS seems to have become, over the last few years, sort of 'fundamentalist Christian', in the sense that they suddenly have decided that it's 'right' to try to make it very 'plain' and 'upfront' when it comes to side-effects of drugs, for example, on the drug notes which are often shown to patients.

Not only that, but from my own previous knowledge, doctors tend to be lousy mathematicians (and in particular, lousy statisticians) – I can recall that the people I knew (at school) who went in for doctoring just about all gave up mathematics at an early stage. For what they seem to be doing is forgetting the fundamental rule of statistics, which is to take full account of other factors which might encroach on 'the situation in hand'.

Probably quite a high percentage of 'serious' tablets have quite a lot of quite serious possible side-effects. This has probably always been known. But they (the NHS) have suddenly decided that these should all be listed for the patients to see. The trouble is that this is apparently being done even when the risk is low (which was never done before, I don't think), and all this is doing is creating very great fear among patients. For example, I know someone who has a fairly serious disorder (but not <u>that</u> serious), who was told that he will probably have a heart attack in 10 years because of his medication. And I'm sure that all this is just basically 'very awful mathematics'.

The situation in mental health, for example, is even worse. I happen to know that some of the drugs they use to treat mental disorders are now thought to have quite horrendous side-effects. And patients are being given the drug notes, which show these, with the result that it almost seems as if you're 'committing suicide' by taking them. Patients are told that they cause heart disease, and lots of other major illnesses.

But I'm sure that all this is basically just unbelievable incompetence on the part of the NHS. All that is actually known is that mental patients tend to die younger. As is well known, people who are comfortably off tend to live longer than those who are poorer – and mentally ill people tend to die sooner than 'ordinary' poor people – that is just a fact of life.

But there are all sorts of reasons for this. For example, a very high percentage of those who are diagnosed with a (serious) mental health problem not only become 'long term unemployed', but <u>never</u> work again (even if they are very young when it happens). That is obviously very unhealthy. A lot of them live on 'junk food'. And psychiatrists and their staff have encouraged mental patients to smoke – or they did until quite recently. Many mental patients more or less chain smoke, at a time when that is now very rare.

Another thing is that mentally ill men are very often made impotent by the drugs that they take. Whether this is deliberate or a coincidence no-one seems to know, but I have my suspicions that it is deliberate, because I also happen to know that quite a few mentally ill women are sterilised.

I'm sure this (either becoming impotent [men] or sterilised [women]) reduces the 'life affirming force' (called the self-actualizing tendency by famous psychologist Carl Rogers) in people, which would probably reduce life expectancy.

Interestingly, someone told me (a male mental patient) that about every 3 years the psychiatric nurses go through a questionnaire with you to see if you have any of the side-effects that the drugs cause. There are about 100 questions. Just about every possible side-effect is mentioned <u>except</u> whether the person has experienced impotency. Instead of this the question asked is whether the person can reach a climax. Now, just about any man can reach a climax, whether they are impotent or not………

This means the NHS hides the fact that a high percentage of men with a mental health problem are made impotent by their medication.

[I know all these things because I had a drink problem, and went into hospital (a mental hospital) because of it. I have written about this elsewhere.]

What Are You Women Complaining About?

Women complain about a lack of 'equality', but in many respects they really lord it over the men.

It may be true that on average, men probably earn more than women.

But think of this:

Back in my twenties I went out with a nurse for a while. And during that time, she invited me to a party at the nurses home. I went, and one of my (male) friends came with me.

And (because in those days nearly all nurses were women – I am not sure if they still are) – at this party there were just us two men – we were the only male contingent –

and there were about 25 women. It was great.

But – this is no word of a lie – that was the <u>only</u> time in my life that anything like that happened. And it was very common for things to be more or less the other way round.

And these days especially, any young woman, in a town like my home town, has the chance of that sort of opportunity (only the reverse, if you see what I mean) – not just once in their life, but <u>every single weekend.</u>

It's true. There are pubs in my home town – pubs for younger people – where you can <u>guarantee</u> that there will be about 10 times as many men as women – and there are no pubs at all where there are almost as many women as men.

So, if they want to, they can experience exactly the same thing (from their point of view) every Friday and Saturday night that I experienced just the once – they can be one of just a few girls in a group of maybe 40 or so men.

What Madness Is This?

What madness is it, that caused those tests for Alzheimer's disease to be invented and for the NHS (apparently) to encourage people to take them (whether one is likely to get the disease in 10 years). Surely that is the last thing any person in their right mind would want to know. To me, it is ridiculous that anyone should recommend people to have this test. The only winners are the insurance companies.

Actually, even for doctors to go to lengths to deliberately look for the early signs seems to me to be rank stupidity. (The author's father died of Alzheimer's disease.)

A Criticism Of What Seems To Be Current Practice In Education – Teachers 'Playing The Psychiatrist'

When I was a child, at school, I believe I am right in saying that teachers virtually never got involved in 'psychology' (I'm actually talking about 'psychological labelling'). Of course, some children were more badly behaved than others, some were more 'highly strung' than others, or more easily upset. That goes without saying. But I believe that teachers almost always deliberately steered clear of making 'medical interpretations'.

And I think that was a very good thing.

But I believe that things may have changed.

I have overheard locally (in a coffee shop actually) teachers talking about children in their charge – the emotional/ mental side of it – using medical terminology and, for various reasons, I think that is very foolish.

Firstly, I think it is very unprofessional to be having discussions like this in coffee shops anyway – who knows who might be listening (people like me, for instance!)

Secondly, with almost certainly a very crowded curriculum regarding teacher training, I doubt whether it can be possible for trainee teachers to have more than a very few lectures on emotional/ mental/ medical subjects regarding children, and I just don't think this would be sufficient at all, to start 'playing the psychiatrist'.

But this is what these teachers, in this coffee shop, appeared to be doing.

Maybe they were mavericks and this was very much the exception.

But if it is now common practice for teachers to get involved in what can only be described as psychiatric labelling of children, then I can only say that I believe that is a step or three too far.

Coffee Shop (Business) Meetings (1)

It seems to be the in thing to hold business meetings, and other types of meetings, in coffee shops (or sometimes pubs). I'm a frequent visitor to coffee shops, as I don't have a full time job anymore – usually in towns fairly near my home town. And I've overheard many meetings that, frankly, I would have thought should have been confidential. (Actually a couple of them are described in this book.)

Interviews, appraisals, discussions about marketing strategy – anything goes. I have been a manager at a large organisation myself, and I would have said that all this is a mark of considerable incompetence.

Coffee Shop (Business) Meetings (2)

As I have been going to a couple of coffee shops a day, for some time, I am a good person to write about this. And I've witnessed countless interviews or appraisals, and lots of meetings about 'company progress' – that sort of thing. The way you can always tell it's a business meeting is that at least 1 of the participants will have a notebook and will be scribbling away for much of the time. Often, if the coffee shop is quite busy, there will be 2 or 3 of these meetings going on at the same time, in different parts of the coffee shop.

Sometimes maybe a couple of managers 'commandeer' a table and they will be sat there all morning, or even practically all day I think, as one after another interviewees arrive, are bought a coffee, and have their interview.

Being An Ex-Member Of A Hampshire Church

(About 25 Years Ago)

For quite a few years I was an evangelical or 'born again' Christian. I was converted when I first went to university, aged 18.

And I must say that at the time I thought it was wonderful to meet people – fellow students, who seemed to have such a vivid and real knowledge of God and Jesus Christ, such as I never had believed was possible. Being told that you could know and love Jesus Christ as if he was your best friend. And that heaven really existed – and that I was going there (providing I didn't 'backslide', which I was taught that some Christians did. But I was sure that wouldn't be me).

At first I hardly noticed that there was a downside – which was that those who didn't believe were equally certainly bound for hell, unless they changed too. This, unfortunately, probably included a lot of people I knew back home.

But I was too busy feeling happy about my new world to feel really bad about that at first. After all, I had the opportunity to try to convert them to Christianity later – I was sure they would be interested when they saw the change in me. I was a bit sad that they weren't at first, though.

Two or three years later I became interested in counselling and applied psychology (psychotherapy etc). I became interested in Encounter groups and primal therapy. I went to some Encounter groups. I read about transactional analysis in the books *'Games People Play'* by Eric Berne and *'I'm OK You're OK'* by Dr Thomas Harris. I was impressed.

I'm OK You're OK was a very good title. In one phrase it encapsulated such a lot about the new lifestyle I was reading about. I didn't realise at the time just how much. It also didn't occur to me to contrast this with what it meant to be a Christian. I realise now that for a keen evangelical Christian, the relationship with a non-Christian, at root, can only be the most extreme form of I'm OK You're not OK – I'm going to heaven and you're going to hell (unless you change).

Dr Harris, in his book I'm OK You're OK, suggests that I'm not OK You're OK is the first tentative decision humans make based on their experiences during the first year of life. Then, by the end of the second year it is either confirmed or it gives way to position 2 or 3 – I'm not OK You're not OK or I'm OK You're not OK. Then, Dr Harris says, once finalised, the child stays in his chosen state and it governs everything he does. It stays with him the rest of his life, unless he later consciously changes it to the fourth position I'm OK You're OK – which is what Dr Harris recommends, and just how to do that is what his book is all about.

I would suggest that something else that could happen is that whatever mode a person is in, if that person gets religious – specifically if they become a 'born again' or evangelical Christian, then at a deep subconscious level they change to the I'm OK You're not OK position, at least when they are relating to non-Christians. From what Dr Harris says, the I'm OK You're not OK state is very destructive.

Because the basic viewpoint of the evangelical Christian towards a non-Christian is this most extreme form of I'm OK You're not OK, I believe evangelical Christianity is basically a very destructive religion. Enough said!

It is over 25 years since I was involved with the church. So in quite a lot of respects I possibly don't really know 'what goes on' these days, like I used to. But I have a feeling that vicars and people don't go on about 'hell' nearly as much as they used to – maybe even hardly ever. I think these days they tend to use other expressions like 'being cut off from God'.

Why Libraries (Apart From Reference Libraries) Are Evil

How would Tesco (in the UK) or Walmart (in the USA) like it if the government opened a store in every city and town, offering the same things, but giving everything away free?

It is because of libraries that books are so ridiculously cheap.

It is because of libraries that most authors earn far less than the minimum wage (unless they have another job).

About Uk Car Manufacturers

I suppose UK car manufacturers can be pleased with themselves that over the last 20 years or so, there have been great improvements in the emissions figures of the cars they sell in the UK. However, as someone who was involved in the motor industry about 35 years ago, I know that it was 'standard practice' that manufacturers exported outdated cars (outdated in the UK), for instance to developing countries.

So is this still happening?

Climate change is a global issue and there is little point in greatly improving the emission figures of cars sold in the UK if manufacturers are still exporting hundreds of thousands of high emissions vehicles every year to less wealthy countries.

Furthermore, there are not going to be any new petrol or diesel engine cars sold in the UK after 2030. But I see that they are still going to be exporting petrol and diesel cars.

The mind boggles at the stupidity and hypocrisy of this.

About Opticians

Not only do dentists give you about 10 times as many X-rays as are necessary (see earlier in this section), but opticians have now started to as well. In just about all the main chains of opticians (I think), an X-ray is included when you have an eye test. This is usually at least every two years.

They tell you they take a picture 'behind the eyes' to detect possible disease. This is, of course, an X-ray. When I complained to an assistant in my opticians that I didn't like having too many X-rays, she said that it wasn't an X-ray – that there was in fact 'a hole in the eye' so they could take a picture without it being an X-ray. This is garbage, I'm sure – something a 5 year old might say, I would have thought. Whether the management told the assistants to give this explanation I'm not really sure.

SECTION 3
Being More Reasonable In Business

A lot about Big Business, and a little about the Press, and the Government (with some controversial ideas).

ARTICLE 1

3 Examples of Being 'Unreasonable' In Business

(1) – 'Social Care'

The 'bosses' in social care are always complaining on TV about their situation, but I want to bring a few anomalies to light.

My mother, while she was alive (until 2019) had 2 or 3 care workers a day visit her, either for 15 minutes or half hour appointments. Because she had some savings, she had to pay. I believe it was about £11 for a 15-minute appointment or about £17 for a half-hour appointment. The care workers told her they got paid only £2 for doing a 15-minute appointment (and I think £4 for a half hour appointment). Many of them didn't have cars and had to walk between appointments. And they weren't paid for this 'walking time'.

Suppose the company had about 150 care workers on their books and about 10 'management staff'. This is what

I've heard might be (approximately) the case for many of these firms. It can clearly be seen that the 'management staff' must be earning a fortune, and probably most of this went to the 2 or 3 owners or directors of the company. You don't need to be a mathematician to see that there are some dreadful inequalities going on here.

Also I have heard from my own brother (regarding my sister-in-law's mother, who is in her nineties and who has dementia), that people* who interviewed her with a view to setting up a "social care package" – "dropped her like a stone" (in my brother's words), when they found out that she rented her property and had no savings (so that the council would have to pay).

From this I would speculate that the problem of "bed-blocking" in hospitals (where elderly people are "medically fit to leave hospital", but cannot leave because a "social care package" cannot be arranged) nearly always happens when the person has no money and when the council would have to pay. When the person has savings and so the social care company can make about a 400% profit (as with my mother), I expect there is <u>no problem at all</u> in arranging a social care package.

* The attempted arranging of a "social care package" (described in the 4th paragraph) may have been by the Council or Social Services, rather than by the Social Care company.

(2) – British Gas

I live in a 1-bedroom flat which has a gas central heating system – a boiler and a few radiators. I'd had a bit of trouble with the boiler, and when I called a plumber on a couple of occasions, they didn't seem to have much knowledge about boilers, and couldn't help me – partly because of this I signed up with British Gas's Homecare Service. This cost about £25 a month, for which I got a service each year, and if I had to call a service engineer out for a problem, I would have to pay an extra £60 for each visit.

Silly me. I thought this was a kind of 'insurance policy' and that more or less whatever went wrong (short of actually needing a new boiler) would be covered by this.

Bear in mind that my previous knowledge in computing (my main technical job before I became self-employed) is well out of date now, and without any other 'trade' any job I got these days would probably be near the minimum wage – so I saw £60 as (in my case) practically a day's work.

But no – when I had a problem with the boiler, I arranged for a service engineer to call (for the £60). He called, and said it was quite a 'big job' and was chargeable. When I got the quote through by email, it was for £840!

[It turned out that it was for what they call a 'power flush'. I did manage to get it done for about half that amount by another heating engineer I found – which seemed to be the going rate for the job (apart from with British Gas). It was about a 3-hour job which I don't think required any parts – it was just labour. The heating engineer that did it told me that British Gas usually contract these jobs out to self-employed plumbers and paid them about £200.]

(3) – The Post Office

Lots of people at the Post Office, at all levels, including at the very top, must have been aware of how, apparently, the 'class' of sub-postmasters had suddenly become a 'highly criminal class'. There had presumably been 20 or so cases of fraud each year during the 60s, 70s, 80s and early 90s (that's a guesstimate – I don't know the exact figures). And then suddenly, from whenever Horizon went on-stream, there were hundreds. You don't need statisticians to tell you that something is very wrong here. Anyone with an IQ of above 70 should have been able to realise that. Come to that, a company as big as the Post Office <u>would</u> certainly have statisticians in their employ. They are trained to treat a 5% difference as 'noticeable and significant'. So, what did they do when they came across a 600% difference (or whatever)? Nothing, apparently.

But anyway – what I have written is obvious to everyone. There is no point in dwelling on it. The main thing I want to talk about in this article is the compensation offered to the thousands of sub-postmasters affected.

Bear in mind that for a lot of them (perhaps most) their lives have been <u>ruined</u> by this. Many went to prison. Quite a few committed suicide, and a number died without knowing they would eventually be exonerated. Even more were bankrupted*. Afterwards they were probably only able to get jobs like cleaning or delivering pizzas – very much jobs at or near the minimum wage, almost certainly with no pension either.

Bear in mind that they had probably looked forward to secure employment with a salary of over £40,000 a year (not just the Post Office salary – most sub-Post Offices were part of a more general shop). They almost certainly would have made provision for a good pension too. All that is gone.

I believe the sort of compensation these people might probably be getting is something like £80,000 to £100,000 (and even that is a long time coming). But I want to say that that will not in any way make up for what they have been through. Their lives have been ruined almost as much as someone who has been in a car crash and is unable to work for the rest of their life. And I believe in that case the compensation would run into millions – which the insurance company has to pay. So, I believe the compensation for the sub-postmasters should be of that order (or at least 1 million). I realise that that would mean that the total compensation paid out by the Post Office would be over a billion pounds. So be it. If the Post Office (now privatised) cannot pay, the government should pay (they should pay anyway, because they owned the Post Office when the scandal happened). And firms losing this amount of money is not unheard of these days. Meta has recently had to pay $725 million. And Volkswagen are having to pay about £26bn for that false emissions claim scandal.

And another thing. As it happens, straight after university, in the late 70s, I worked for GEC Telecommunications on a very big contract they had with the Post Office. It was called System X and was the digitalisation of the telephone network. I was one of hundreds of software engineers working on it at GEC. (And there were also hundreds at Plessey.) This was for Post Office Telecommunications, which was later to become B.T. when it was privatised, sometime in the 80s.

And I do remember that with this enormous project, the Post Office was extremely 'hands on'. They never let you forget that they were the boss. I left within 2 years, while I was still a junior programmer, but I remember that the Section Leaders (who might have been in charge of about 6 software engineers), were very frequently visited by Post Office 'experts' who wanted to know <u>exactly</u> what was going on. I believe it was at least once a fortnight that a Post Office 'expert' visited each of the Section Leaders, and I think it was usually for the full day. You could always tell when a Section Leader was going to be visited by Post Office staff. They would be dressed in a suit, whereas normally they were very scruffily dressed, usually in jeans. There were also very numerous meetings attended by several Post Office employees, and a similar number of GEC employees. And even the programming language we used, which was a so-called 'real-time' programming language (more complicated than a 'standard' programming language like Cobol) was called POCoral – the PO stood for Post Office – it had been specially designed by Post Office experts.

I'm telling you all this because I just don't believe what the Post Office is trying to imply – that the Horizon program was completely designed by Fujitsu, and as far as the Post Office was concerned it was just a 'black box'. Far from it, I expect. I wouldn't be at all surprised if Post Office staff were intimately involved with the design of Horizon, as they were with System X, and so the Post Office itself must take a big share of the blame for the faults in the system.

* In the case of victims of this scandal who went bankrupt, when they receive compensation (particularly if it's a relatively low compensation of £80,000 to £100,000), a large part of this, possibly as much as 90%, will be 'clawed back' by the 'Official Receiver' (See 'Private Eye' magazine No. 1588 (16 Dec. – 5 Jan. 2023))

ARTICLE 2

The Secret of Those "Permanent Half-Price Sales" and More Info on Consuming to Make One's Blood Boil!

Those "permanent half-price sales" - it's all a big con, you know.

The motive behind the con is this.

It's well known in marketing that the public won't often respond to a sale where things are marked down by 10% or 15% - very few more of the goods will be bought than at the original selling price.

But the public usually will respond where the price cutting is around 50% - very often 2, 3 or even 4 or more times as many of the product may be sold.

So that is the motive. How do they do it?

I believe the secret is what in business is called "vertical integration". This is when a retailer or manufacturer buys up some of their suppliers. (It works in the other direction too – like when a manufacturer buys shops to sell his goods in.)

So, where's the connection between this and "permanent half-price sales"?

I believe it is this.

These firms that are always advertising on TV with their offers that sound so marvellous – it's not like the owner had won a couple of million on the lottery, and decided to set up a large retailing business, and wrote to a few manufacturers for details of their products.

It's not like the manufacturers responded to his request with a catalogue and price lists with the retail prices down one column and the wholesale prices down another.

In practice, I'm pretty sure, these large retailers (in certain trades) virtually own the manufacturers they deal with. So, effectively, they set their own retail prices.

And of course, noting that the public will respond to things reduced by 50%, but not to goods at only 15% off, they set the retail prices accordingly.

It's a bit hard on some traditional firms, who do send off to manufacturers for price lists, though. Typically, they may only get 30% or 35% off the retail price as commission, so their sales can look pretty lame – and it's largely because of the prevalence, in some industries, of these permanent half-price sales – I believe – that the public will no longer respond to less attractive sounding offers.

(CHANGING THE SUBJECT)

I have been reading the famous book *"The World is Flat"* by Pulitzer prize-winning author Thomas L Friedman. He is a journalist at the New York Times. This was the book to read a few years ago when it came out, and one of the most talked about. It claims that the turn of the Millennium heralded a new era in the "globalisation stakes" and gives the author's views on that. (He had previously written another book about globalisation up to just before the Millennium, called *"The Lexus and the Olive Tree: Understanding Globalisation"* - published in 1999.)

"The World is Flat" certainly opened my eyes about some of the issues of globalisation.

It seems that with the lower wage rates in India and China, hardly any of our jobs are safe, even (or indeed, especially) the jobs of professionals. Any type of work that could in some way be "digitised" could be farmed out to an organisation in India or China and performed for a much lower cost than would be possible in America (or Britain). He gave as one of many examples the completion of tax forms – accountancy was one of many professions where jobs certainly aren't safe.

Both India and China are building (or have built) a superb educational system. Their many universities (the elite ones anyway) are arguably superior to most of those in the West. They are particularly hot on engineering and computer science subjects.

But it was the wage rates of the graduates from these universities (and other high achievers) that really amazed me. Just to give a couple of examples.

1) (Quote from *"The World is Flat"*)

"There are about seventy thousand accounting grads in India each year, (L Gary Boomer) added, many of whom go to work for local Indian firms starting at $100 per month."

(L Gary Boomer is a CPA [that's equivalent to a Charted Accountant in the UK] and writes in the journal "Accounting Today".)

2) Call Centre Workers

Friedman's book says call centre workers – who not only have to speak English (or American) fluently, but also learn various regional accents, so that it seems that they are in the region from which the phone call is placed – are regarded as the elite (even more than accounting grads).

The pay of workers at 24/7, a very large call centre operation in India, starts at $200 per month. (You can tell how much of an "elite" job this is, by the fact that the 24/7 call centre gets about seven hundred applications a day and only 6% - about 40 – of them are hired.)

$100 per month is £65.20 per month or £15.05 per week. $200 per month is £130.40 or £30.10 per week (exchange rates at 22/9/11).

Remember that, as I said, the people who get these jobs, at these rates, are the elite. So, goodness knows how low the wage rates must be for more "ordinary" jobs, for example (factory) manufacturing jobs.

Perhaps an ordinary manufacturing worker would earn about £10 - £12 per week – that seems feasible. It makes you wonder, with figures like these (and also when you think of what can be bought from places like Poundland for £1), just how many of the goods we buy from shops in the UK for between, say, £70 and £200, were bought by traders or the buyers in large chain stores for perhaps between £5 and £10!

Note: Whilst the press will sometimes expose individual "one-off" rip-offs, they probably wouldn't want to expose whole sections of marketing practice, because that would most likely considerably affect their advertising revenues – many papers probably make more money from their advertising than from the sale of the papers themselves.

ARTICLE 5
About Private Equity Firms

There has been a lot of talk in the press about Private Equity Firms, but most people still don't know that much about them.

Private Equity Firms buy and sell whole companies. The deals are so huge – they have been able to raise so much money – that at one time practically no UK firm was too big to be a Private Equity "target."

Typically, about a fifth or a quarter of the cost of a firm will come from the Private Equity Firm's investment fund, and the rest will be borrowed from a bank (or banks).

Most of the income Private Equity firms make is due to the Capital Gains that they make when they sell a business they have previously bought.

The investment fund is what is increased when a company is sold for a profit, but typically 20%* of this profit is kept by the Private Equity firm – it is what is known as the "carry".

One example of a well-known UK firm being bought by

Private Equity was Alliance Boots (owners of Boots the chemist). At the beginning of 2007 it was bought by just about the most famous US Private Equity firm – Kohlberg Kravis Roberts (KKR) – for £11.1 billion. £9 billion of this was borrowed from banks.

The way it all works is this. Suppose the private equity firm buys a company for £10 billion, of which £8 billion is borrowed. Then £2 billion is provided by the Private Equity firm's investment fund. This isn't the Private Equity firm's own money, but is similar to a unit trust – it is provided by investors. If the Private Equity firm goes on to sell the company for £13 billion after, say 3 years, the "equity" (a similar idea to the equity in a house) has grown from £2 billion to £5 billion. i.e. £2 billion has produced £3 billion profit. The Private Equity firm will keep 20% of this profit* (the "carry") - so in this case £600 million is what the Private Equity firm itself earns from the deal.

[Typically, most of this £600 million will go to just a very few (perhaps 2-5) "senior partners" in the Private Equity firm. No wonder the Private Equity business boasts quite a few multi-billionaires (especially in America). And what is more, because the New Labour government (of 1997 – 2010) was keen to "keep on the right side" of these people – they believed it was good for the country that they stayed in the UK – they introduced extremely favourable tax treatment for them. It can be seen that this £600 million is really the Private Equity firm's income – but it would not be taxed as income (which would attract a 40% rate), but at a special low rate (10%

recently increased – because of a public outcry – to 18%) of Capital Gains Tax.]

How the Private Equity firm aims to make that £3 billion (or whatever) profit in selling the company they've bought, after perhaps 3 years, is usually by instigating a ruthless efficiency drive in the company, so that overheads are dramatically lowered, and profits increase. (This will tend to increase the value of the company.)

Typically, they will do this (partly) by getting many of the lower paid workers to significantly increase their "productivity" whilst paying them hardly anything more per hour worked.

No wonder unions campaign against Private Equity deals.

Another thing that many people would think unfair, concerning these Private Equity firms, is that the firms they take on tend to pay much less Corporation tax than an equivalent public company.

This is because of the huge amounts of borrowing that is undertaken – as we have seen it can be as much as £9 billion. Obviously there is then a large amount of interest to be paid to the bank, and under current tax law this can be claimed against the Corporation tax due.

So - many businesses, having been bought by Private Equity firms, from then on pay hardly any Corporation tax, or even are paid tax credits from the taxman if the interest payment is high enough.

And a common way in which the assets of a business a Private Equity firm buys are plundered, is that they immediately sell off the freehold properties that the business owns (to specialist companies) – and then lease them back. This "frees" capital.

Private Equity firms tend to be secretive about this figure. 20% is Robert Peston's estimate of a typical figure. (Robert Peston is an ITV financial commentator and author of "Who Runs Britain".)

ARTICLE 4

Heading Towards Authoritarianism and Other Negatives

25 years or so ago, everyone was saying that with increased automation we all wouldn't need to work so hard in a few years. Everyone would have vastly increased leisure time. But it hasn't happened, has it?

Oh, there's more automation, alright. But despite this, it seems to me that on average, people have to work <u>harder</u>, and there's <u>more stress</u>, and believe it or not for <u>less reward</u> (relatively speaking).

Let me explain how I come to these conclusions.

Some years ago most wives didn't go out to work – the husband would usually be the only breadwinner in the family. Now it is usual for both partners in a relationship to work. So that means straight away that nearly twice as much "work" is being done. So much for increased automation meaning we all have to work less.

Secondly, from what I see around me, my view is that people generally are much worse off than they were 30 years ago.

I'll explain why I say that.

Noting the current situation and remembering what it was like 30+ years ago when I was a young man, I think that whereas it was common for young people to go out almost every night, now hardly anyone goes out for more than 2 nights a week – therefore most people must be significantly worse off these days.

I was saying that I believe there is so much more stress now, too. I'll just give a few examples.

All these new call centres. Working in one of these is a common type of job, isn't it? - you're always seeing vacancies in the windows of recruitment agents.

When I was young, so far as I remember it, being some sort of telephonist was often a bit of a doddle. The person would be sat there, and the phone might only ring every 10 minutes or so.

But these call centres are completely different, aren't they? When you ring one up of a major firm, 9 times out of 10 you get music playing and a voice saying that all operators are busy.

That can only mean that they employ just enough

staff so that the operators are talking on the phone virtually the whole time – 8 hours a day non-stop phone conversations. That is completely different from sitting there and the phone ringing every ten minutes.

Secondly, also related to call centres. All these big firms that advertise always tell you "Your call may be recorded". I may be wrong, but I'm pretty sure that usually means <u>all calls</u> are recorded.

But, for a call operator, that must be like having a supervisor looking over your shoulder the whole time you're working.

For at any time a customer may make some sort of complaint, and presumably the recorded call will be played back. And – this is another thing – I've noticed that a lot of firms aren't very forgiving – if the operator has made a mistake, said the wrong thing, there would be serious consequences for them. Like I said, it is like having a supervisor looking over your shoulder the whole time.

Moving on now.

Cleaners and people doing related jobs have always had low status and been badly paid. But there used to be advantages too.

I remember the time when "the cleaner" would usually be a "happy go lucky" person without any worries or responsibilities, who would spend more time chatting than actually doing any work. In short, he would be a bit of a skiver, but no-one really looked down on him for that, in fact he was usually pretty well liked.

Haven't things changed?

These days, I'm pretty sure, even the cleaners are bombarded with "mission statements" and "company goals" and are expected to work their socks off – as it seems to be for everyone now, high or low.

Talking about how people with those sorts of jobs had a reputation for "skiving" - I have a funny story related to that.

When I was a student I had a vacation job for a few weeks with a large organisation that had its main administration building near where I lived.

For part of the time, I was attached to the "maintenance section". It didn't seem to me like much maintenance got done there – most of their job seemed to be preparing the conference rooms, of which there were several, for any conferences or meetings.

And there usually wasn't enough work to keep us busy the whole day. And during a slack period, the man I was working with, who was a bit of a laugh, would say "I know what we'll do – come with me".

It was largely open-plan offices, but there were partitions erected in different places to give sections a bit of privacy.

And this man (and I) would go to where he knew there was one of the best-looking young women in the place (there were a lot of very attractive young women in their twenties working there). And he would take a partition down next to her, and then put it up again, just so we could talk to her. That's how he would spend his quiet periods.

I told this story a couple of years ago to someone I know, who happens to be a manager at the same place now. And I could tell that he was quite shocked. From his reaction, I could tell that nothing like that would happen in a million years now.

And I think that for a long time now, the workplace for so many of us has changed from being quite benign (25 or 30 years ago) to today heading towards having similarities with the nineteenth century and early twentieth century world of the "big bad Robber Barons" - with the management having more power than they know what to do with. And in all sorts of ways things are getting much more authoritarian than they were.

One last point. We have certainly moved into a computer age. But in some ways, and for some people, it appears to be a retrograde step. In my time I have sometimes had to do quite boring work. But there's one type of job I wouldn't accept in a million years. And that is as a data input clerk – repetitively putting into a computer a succession of numbers via a keyboard. That kind of work would be mental torture for me and I'd never last a day! I'd put it on a par, for boredom and monotony, with cleaning a floor with a toothbrush – apparently one of the punishments they used to give you in the army as an alternative to "jankers".

And yet in this wonderfully exciting "computer age" I believe data input clerk is one of the commonest unskilled jobs around.

Most of us only have 70 or 80 odd years on this earth (some less), and I believe it is an act of treason to humanity to employ people for this sort of work for any length of time – and would be at £30 an hour, let alone near the minimum wage.

Note: A great many people would love to start their own business. But the way things are, it is becoming increasingly difficult for people to do that successfully, as this next article explains. Therefore this, again, is something that is making a lot of people angry (even if, like a lot of the anger, it is largely unconscious).

ARTICLE 5

Big Vs Small
As Regards Company Size

I know that quite a large percentage of people, even with very good jobs, dream of starting their own business.

I think there must be something intrinsically more pleasurable about working for a small company with, say, a dozen employees, than a corporate giant with 30,000.

In the small firm everyone knows exactly how their contribution "makes a difference", and I believe there is fulfilment in that.

And yet, in all sorts of ways, in modern society (in Britain anyway) things seem to be so much in favour of the big firm. This article will describe some of the ways that this is so.

First of all, I'll take my own case as an example. (A few times I have started my own business – so I have a bit of relevant knowledge.)

When you start a business one of the most important

things is to somehow let your potential customers know of your "offer".

Being a small firm, as far as I could see I really had only 3 options:

1) A regular small advert in the weekly local paper.

2) A "leaflet drop" in the area.

3) Some sort of mailshot to people on a relevant (targeted) mailing list.

And these are basically the options for quite a lot of small local businesses.

But – do you see where this is leading? - these are precisely the approaches that are getting more and more out of favour with the public.

Leaflet drops and direct mail (sending a letter to people on a mailing list) in particular – I'm sure as each year goes by, a smaller proportion of people even glance at these.

It's incredibly difficult (just about impossible in many cases) to make a profit if it's the case that only 2 people in 100 (probably), are even looking at that leaflet you're delivering to each house in the area, or reading the letter you're sending through the post. (That "statistic" was quoted in a marketing book I read – I'm not sure how accurate it is.)

Of course, large firms use direct mail and what are effectively leaflet drops too. I'm not sure what level of success they have. But I sometimes think it is a concerted effort by the large firms to keep up a constant barrage of this "junk mail" just so that it will scupper the chances of any small firms making headway – I'm sure one of the fears of large organisations is that new competition will appear "out of nowhere" i.e. a new small firm "making good".

What I'm saying is that this increasing trend of throwing anything that looks like "junk mail" immediately into the bin is one of the things that is advantageous to large firms as opposed to small firms – or rather, I should say it is more disadvantageous to small firms, because they have fewer options – if you take away the cost-effectiveness of direct mail or a leaflet drop, in many cases the firm is scuppered.

Larger firms, of course, have other options, like radio advertising, or in the case of much larger ones, TV advertising.

As a possible remedy to the situation, the only thing I can think of is to suggest that firms shouldn't be allowed to use both TV advertising and direct mail – one or the other, but not both. This would stop householders being swamped by so many mailshots from large firms who, in any case, have other options that they can use.

The other remedy, of course, is the responsibility of the public themselves.

I think this trend in attitudes that almost seems to suggest that any small firm that uses direct mail is on the way to being a crook – that almost seems to be it – is very unfortunate.

As more and more people throw anything away that "smells" of "junk mail" with barely a glance, more and more small firms, who might well have had a lot to offer, had a good attitude, and only wanted to be allowed to do what they had trained to do, are having to call in the receivers.

If anything, I think it is the large firms, often with a very good reputation, who more than any others are misusing the medium.

I think, for these reasons, we really have a duty to at least see what offer these firms are making – this doesn't mean reading every letter from top to bottom – if something is not at all relevant to you, you can usually tell this by the second or third line, and then it can go in the bin.

That covers what I want to say about leaflet drops and direct mail.

For my own businesses I've often used the free distribution papers. It's true that using them is the only way you can get an advert into a very large number of homes (sometimes as many as 150 000) for as little as twenty quid – though I had little success with extremely small ads (you only get about a 10-word lineage ad for £20 typically) – and I tended to buy £80 or £100 ads fortnightly, which for me was more cost-effective.

Of course, just because the paper has a circulation of 150 000 doesn't mean that that many people are going to read your £80 ad – I actually think only a very small percentage will – that's what you can assume.

But for various reasons I don't want to say much, either pro or con, about this advertising medium. After all, I may well be using it again to try to sell my books!

But I think that, pound for pound, TV advertising is probably a considerably more cost-effective advertising medium than the papers. After all, people may typically spend only 10 minutes a day reading the paper, but many spend several hours in front of the TV virtually every evening. And for TV advertisers, viewers are really a captive audience. Since it is only large firms that can afford TV advertising, this increased cost-effectiveness for this type of advertising again works in favour of large firms.

Regarding the papers though – and so-called "print-advertising" - there is obviously a whole different attitude towards it than there was in days gone by.

A hundred years ago, for instance, I believe the trend was to have "wordy" adverts that looked more like a journalistic piece. Even thirty years ago there was very often quite a bit of very important "body copy".

These days it almost seems that every advert has to be 7 words or less (sometimes only 3 words). Sometimes there is smaller text too, but it is often clear that not many people are expected to read this – the whole message is got across in those 6 or 7 words.

An advert can only effectively say "remember me – yes of course you do" (or maybe announce a sale or something) in 6 or 7 words. These things are not much help if you are a new or unknown (small) company.

I think overall there is an unfortunate lack of much (advertising) that is "local", in fact. Just about all magazines have a national distribution which virtually forces any specialised firm (where a specialised magazine is usually the best advertising medium) to "go national" very quickly. As I say later I don't necessarily think this is a good thing at all.

But again, this obviously works against small local companies.

A large company might have a million or more customers, whereas a small one only about 1000. Suppose both companies were in the same field. If both did similar advertising, (and similarly expensive) the cost of the advertising to each customer reached, is <u>1000 times greater</u> to the small company than to the large one – this obviously works <u>massively</u> to the advantage of the large company (and is one of the reasons why direct mail is popular with relatively small firms).

Now I want to talk about the apparent need for firms to get big if they can.

First of all, a little diversion.

Relating to the lottery, I've heard quite a few people say that they don't know why they have to have just one big prize of a few million – wouldn't it be better to have at least 10 or 20 times as many smaller prizes of £100 000 or £150 000?

Personally, I don't really agree with this. If a typical family won £100 000 to £120 000, say, it would obviously make them more "comfortable", but it wouldn't be enough to really change their life – they probably wouldn't be able to give up their jobs, for instance.

It probably would take at least a million these days to make jacking your job in and retiring to Spain or somewhere an option – which surely is what it's all about.

But what I want to say is that I think it's different for firms.

When a person starts a firm (it's quite often just one person or not more than 2 or 3) the chances are the ambition is to become as big as possible. It is true that if a business "works" in one town it is quite likely to work in many towns.

But just because you've started a clothes shop, say, in Winchester that's doing quite well, doesn't mean that society would benefit much if there were 500 of these shops, one in most towns in the country.

And yet that's the impression you would get sometimes. So many firms want to expand as greatly as they possibly can.

But I said at the beginning of this article that there is more "intrinsic pleasure" - more fulfilment possible with working for a small firm than with a big one.

Actually, this "urge to expand" often works against the entrepreneurs that start the firm in the first place.

There comes a point (size-wise) where a firm isn't best run by an "entrepreneurial" type of person – he (or she) will just find themselves out of their depth. It takes more the qualities of a computer programmer, probably, than an entrepreneur, to run a really big firm. Time after time entrepreneurs have set firms up, they have become successful and expanded. But at a certain point, even though it continued to be successful, they've had to sell out – basically to accountants I expect – because they didn't have all the degrees in management science, at the end of the day.

I read a book a couple of years ago, about starting up and running a small business based on an internet web site. And the author said that the way you had to look at things was this.

There is a very big wall in Jerusalem (probably a famous one) made from massive stones. And in between some of these stones were little crevices, perhaps with moss growing – I think that's what the author said.

And he said that (if we're thinking of starting a business) we've got to forget the massive stones – the "big jobs" in other words - "mass market products" if you like.

Because in most cases there were a few big firms that basically would wipe the floor with you if you tried to get in there and make an impression. Instead, you had to look to the little crevices, the tiny little openings that nobody else had thought of, and the big firms wouldn't be interested in … And I thought that was rather sad, really.

I really think it would be good if all these advantages for large firms were reversed, or at least made less severe.

ARTICLE 6
The Ludicrous Housing Situation

This article was written in about 2009 (but it's still relevant in 2023).

A) The Ridiculous Price Of Housing - Bought Or Rented

About 9 years ago (I think it was) the interest rates on mortgages were roughly halved – from about 10% to about 5%. This was something to do with coming in line with the rest of Europe, I believe.

House prices had been going up way above inflation for years and many families were spending around half their income on the mortgage, which was totally ridiculous in my opinion. With this reduction in the interest rate it was surely an opportunity for nearly everyone to end up paying much less (maybe 40% less – something like that), leaving much more to spend on other things – surely a beneficial outcome.

But no – thanks to the "herd instinct", within four or five years house prices had massively increased (by about 50% - and had doubled within about a decade), so that those buying a house, either for the first time or moving up the property ladder – were probably still paying a ludicrously high percentage of their income on the mortgage.

I think the government should have done something to prevent this (doubling of the prices of houses) – from happening. The government many years ago introduced legislation to restrict the rise in rents of rented property. Obviously, a similar sort of initiative (legislation to restrict house price increases) would be practically impossible, I should think. In actual fact, I believe reintroducing restrictions to the rise in rents of rental property would probably have the desired effect of reversing the seemingly never-ending hike in house prices, especially for first-time buyer properties – which would help our young people looking to get on the property ladder. (Of course, not everyone wants house prices to come down – but that's another story.)

This is because rent restrictions would make the buy-to-let market less desirable, and so bring down the price of typical buy-to-let properties. But these properties are also typically first-time buyer houses. In other words, as buy-to-let landlords leave the market, their properties would become available again to first-time buyers – there would be less competition for them.

And of course, the high percentage of young people who rent their homes, unable to afford to buy, would be directly helped too.

In my view it is very dangerous to allow house prices to rise as they have done – not just recently, but over the last 25 years (and especially over the last 12). If the mortgage rate reverts to being about 10% again, a significant number of people will be effectively bankrupted.

More about the unhealthy trends

When I started my working life about 30 years ago, my rent was a very small proportion of my earnings (which were typical earnings for someone newly out of university). Two or three years later the mortgage on the first house I owned was, again, very low.

This is what we should be returning to, so that people have money in their pockets to spend on "non-essentials" like going out in the evenings. But instead, we are moving in the opposite direction. Even housing associations who provide "social housing" are rushing to make their rents catch up with those in the private sector, with increases of 15% per annum being quite typical in many places.

B) Some Criticisms Of The Building Industry (And Estate Agents)

Regarding this tremendous rise in house prices – a proportion of houses are new and I cannot understand what is happening here. Have building materials, and the wages of workers in the building industry also been going up way above inflation for the last dozen years at least? That's one possibility. But it seems to me that some people (perhaps the owners of building firms, perhaps the owners of land) – have been siphoning off an awful lot of excess money.

Back in the days when the unions were stronger, one of their main jobs was establishing "pay differentials" between different types of worker. The idea was that a job which required more skill, more training, would offer higher pay. Or where the working conditions were less appealing for whatever reason. It didn't just work like that though. Some unions had great power through the threat, or the actuality of strike action, and these were the ones who generally got the best deals for their workers.

Times change and these days it seems the workers who do best aren't necessarily those in the strongest unions (there aren't many strong unions left, compared to the old days). But now the thing is for your firm's products to be of "premium value". And since a greater and greater proportion of the average family's expenditure has gone on the mortgage or rent, so that now, as I said, it is often over half of total income, no "product" has had more "premium value" than the family home.

So probably, using these arguments, it is building workers who have moved to the top of the financial heap among the working classes. And fair play to them, I suppose.

There is however, one particular criticism I have of building firms in general, and also of another related occupation – estate agents. It is obvious that for most of the time, building firms, and estate agents, must have done exceptionally well in the last dozen years (or in fact even longer).

For example, estate agents' fees are based on a percentage of the selling price of the property – so when property prices doubled, their income doubled too (assuming they sold just as many houses, which they probably did).

But it is well known in the property market that you do occasionally have a bad year. There was one in 1990, and this last year has been pretty dreadful for them (2008/9).

But why on earth don't these firms prepare themselves for the possibility of having bad years? They have been so lucky most of the time. But it seems they don't do any such thing – when they have the occasional bad year, when property prices go down and therefore stop selling in the same numbers, we see both builders and estate agents going broke in droves.

In my (smallish) hometown, there are about four now empty shops all in one street, which used to be estate agents – the result of having a bad year*. It seems laughable to me that they are in this position, after so many what must have been extremely good years.

* *To be fair, I don't think these estate agents went broke – or certainly not all of them. Some of them were probably part of large chains; but there was certainly a lot of "consolidation" - and a few of them popped up elsewhere in town in more secondary positions.*

**The downturn probably considerably affected the advertising revenues of local papers too – in my local paper (which I think is typical) there are pages and pages taken up by estate agents, and I expect that was one of the first things that was cut back.*

ARTICLE 7
Why Doesn't Anyone Go For A Walk Any More?

There are quite a few footpaths and the like near where I live, and I quite often go for a walk just "for the sake of it" - at least twice a day usually. And I find it one of my most productive times for thinking. Not just ideas for articles – though that is one thing, certainly. But also, for example, working out in my mind what I'm going to say in a phone call.

On these walks – which can be at any time of the day – I quite often pass people coming in the opposite direction. But there's one thing I've noticed. They've nearly always got a dog with them. Either that, or it's between 8 and 9 in the morning, or around 5 in the evening, and it's very obvious that they're going to or from work.

What I'm saying is that hardly anyone these days goes for a walk just "for the sake of it" - there always has to be a reason or an excuse.

And I just wonder why that is.

I haven't read much classic literature, but from what I have read, for instance nineteenth century novels by the

Brontë sisters and George Eliot – I'm sure from what I remember it was very common for the protagonists to go for a walk, when, for instance, they wanted to think.

But apparently it doesn't happen anymore.

There are certain other times I find conducive to thinking – having a bath or shower, or lying on the bed, for instance.

But funny enough, the one place I can just about guarantee I won't have any new, original ideas is if I deliberately sit down at my desk with that goal in mind i.e. to "have an idea".

I've had quite a few jobs that involved a lot of thinking e.g. my "technical posts" for telecommunications companies, and I've read about quite a few more – for instance I've read books about copywriting.

And the thing that's struck me in both cases was that just like for any other job, you were expected to sit at your desk for virtually the whole day – that's where you had to come up with your ideas.

[In one of the books about copywriting I read, which was partly almost autobiography, the author writes about having his feet on the table half the time and talking with his partner about the movies – his partner would be an artist – there would usually be teams of a copywriter and art director (artist) in an advertising agency. But the fact remains, he is still at his desk nearly all the time.]

And I really think that firms might well get more out of their "creative people" if they weren't expected to spend most of their time at the office.

What are firms afraid of in any case? Is it that these creative types won't put in enough work? That they'll skive off?

But it's all a bit ridiculous really. Pop stars love talking about their famous song that they wrote in 10 minutes, don't they?

Surely it really isn't a question of how many hours and minutes an employee "puts in" that counts, when we're talking about jobs like these, but the quality of work that's produced.

ARTICLE 8
Do You Speak Japanese?

A few years ago, I took a job at an engineering factory.

One thing there that attracted my attention was that plastered all over the walls of the place were, instead of paintings or something aesthetic like that, all sorts of graphs about company progress – how many components had been made in the last month etc. As well as this, also on the walls was information about things like Japanese management techniques (and I believe they made components for Japanese firms, amongst others).

I've read quite a few books about business and marketing, and in a lot of them are details about Japanese management techniques.

Some of them are fairly simple, others not so.

But the thing that amused me at this factory, was that (as far as I can remember) practically all this information on the walls about Japanese management techniques was about the one called "kaizen" - which simply means "progress by continuous improvement". It's so simple that even a 5-year-old could understand it.

In fact, how the Japanese have managed to accomplish the task of claiming (largely successfully) that it _is_ a Japanese management technique I don't really know. I should have thought just about every business that's been started, for hundreds of years, that wasn't an exact copy of something that's already existed, would have used it.

I was certainly using it myself in my businesses before I read that it had been "invented" by the Japanese and called "kaizen" - for example, whatever I did, it was the case that my advertising material had to get better results, and I did that <u>by a process of continuous improvement</u> – that was the way I worked. As I said, that was before I found out it had a name. I just assumed that everyone did that.

Anyway, I was saying that practically all the information on the walls was about this "kaizen".

And really, I thought it was very patronising that they should have chosen to major to such an extent on this technique that is, as I said, so ridiculously simple.

ARTICLE 9
A suggestion for the government

Note: This article was written in about 2010.

The Government (of whatever hue, since *"New Labour"* replaced *"Old Labour"*), seems scared stiff to offend very wealthy people, for example the elite in the City*. One of the reasons for this is surely that both the Labour party and the Conservative party rely on donations from very wealthy people.

For example, Robert Peston (in his book *"Who Runs Britain"*, mentions several donations to New Labour by bosses of private equity firms or hedge funds, ranging from £510,000 to £1.8M. In the scheme of things (compared to the mega-sums bandied about relating to the banking industry in recent months, for instance), these are not really enormous amounts. (You would be lucky to buy 3 houses with £510,000, in many areas.) Surely rather than allowing these donations to influence policies, often in negative ways (in ways that detract from the "common good"), it would be better if the main parties were financed out of taxpayers' money – perhaps each of the 3 main parties receiving, say, £12M – and that donations of the above-mentioned type were banned.

In December 2009 the Labour government did get tough with the City elite. But this was either an aberration, or a last-ditch effort to garner some votes for the 2010 election.

Note: I wanted quite a large article to show how a group of the population with a lot more than average talent, were being "downtrodden" in modern Britain – to give emphasis to my subtitle. I had an article about writers – most people now know how abysmally a lot of writers are paid. But then I remembered that I also had an article about musicians, and for various reasons, I've decided to use that instead.

ARTICLE 10

Let's Give Singers And Musicians Who Aren't Famous A Chance

*This article (partly about my hometown) relates mainly to what was happening 4-6 years ago (between 2009 and 2011) and is not quite so relevant to what is the situation now, in 2015. For instance, since the government's cuts, I believe the subsidy at the Lights (an entertainment venue in Andover) has been drastically cut (it may even have been removed altogether) – and this venue no longer has such impressive or well-known acts.

A) Many People Will Only Go To See Bands / Singers If They Are Famous On The Radio / Tv. Contrast This With My Approach.

I find this fact – that so many people are only interested in seeing an act – a band or a singer for instance, if they are on the TV or radio – very annoying.

I personally am very unlikely to hear a band on the radio or see them on TV simply because actually, I only very rarely either listen to the radio or watch TV.

I started going a lot to "The Lights" in Andover and "The Anvil" in Basingstoke (which are theatres/ entertainment centres) several years ago. I was often going a couple of times a week for much of the year. (This was until about 3 years ago, since when I have got out of the habit, and have been spending my money on other forms of entertainment.)

So, my approach would be to look through the brochures that the Lights and the Anvil both produced, to see what was on over the next 3 weeks or so that I fancied (I rarely booked more in advance than that). Since both the Lights and the Anvil usually had maybe 3 events a week – and these were often Friday and/or Saturday, as I wanted to go to usually 2 events per week, it meant going to quite a high proportion of the events that were on offer. Fortunately, most of the events on offer did seem, from the blurb in the brochures, to be highly "attractive" - and also, I was rarely disappointed when I went.

But one thing I remember is the following. I booked to see Clare Teal, the jazz singer, at the Lights. From the brochure it was clear she had very impressive credentials indeed. For instance, she signed the biggest ever recording deal by a British jazz singer, was a BBC radio 2 personality, and was voted "Jazz Vocalist of the Year" 3 years running.

And when I bought my ticket the lady at the box office wondered whether I knew Clare Teal from the radio. And it was clear from her intonation that she thought that was by far the most likely reason I would want to see her. In other words that that was the reason most people were going to see her – because she was a presenter on the radio. Now of course I hadn't heard her on the radio – to my mind she sounded so good just from the brochure that it would be difficult not to place a "tick" beside that entry when planning what to book. But it seems this method isn't good enough for most people.

Another time, I saw "Bill Wyman and his Rhythm Kings", who were also excellent (this was at the Anvil). And at the end of the performance, one of the members of the group, a singer, gave quite a long speech, a bit of an impassioned plea, for people to buy their CDs, which were on sale at the back of the theatre – because, she said "they just don't play their kind of music on the radio". She made it clear that that was a <u>really</u> big disadvantage and meant that the band was actually struggling. (I realise that these examples I'm giving are turning out to be about people who <u>are</u> famous – still, the point I am making is clear, I think.)

This next example is slightly related – it shows how the success of an artiste is so clearly bound up with whether they are on TV. The artiste is Alesha Dixon.

After finding fame in the all-female trio Mis-Teeq, they separated and Alesha tried to continue as a solo singer. She signed to Polydor Records. But due to poor sales of her first two singles from her debut solo album, *Fired Up*, Polydor Records dropped her. That was in 2006.

But then in 2007 she became a contestant on *Strictly Come Dancing* and won the competition. As a result, she was signed by Warner Music Group and her second solo album *The Alesha Show* (2008) went platinum in the UK. The success of her third album was also assured when she became a judge of *Strictly Come Dancing*.

B) About Recorded Music Being Played In Coffee Shops, Cafes (And Other Shops)

As an adolescent (15 or 16 years old) I worked for a supermarket as a "Saturday boy" and one thing I remember was that though the supermarket played "piped music", and liked to play the "current hits", they weren't allowed to play the "actual" hits (the songs by the famous bands and singers). They had to play tapes which had the same songs, but were recorded by other artists (who were nearly always considerably inferior in quality).

Perhaps this was because of copyright laws, or some restrictions imposed by the Musicians Union – something like that.

Now it looks like the Musicians Union has "gone asleep at the wheel", because nothing like these restrictions apply at all for anyone, it seems.

Virtually any shop seems to be able to play any recorded music it feels like (including the original tracks). I do know that shops like coffee shops have to pay for a license to play whatever recorded music they like, but the amount really is a joke.

I know that some of the busy coffee shop takings are in the region of £50,000 a month, but all they have to pay for the license is something like £7 a week, I believe (it depends on the number of seats). I'm not even sure that this money goes to the musicians anyway.

So, what is going on? Why are all these commercial organisations able to take advantage of the best musical talent there is more or less for free?

[And after all, the music played on the stereo of, say, a coffee shop is probably one of the biggest influences when it comes to defining the "ambiance" - a very valuable thing in cafes and coffee shops – certainly the well-known ones, I would say, have chosen their own "trademark" type of music that they play, and I'm sure their executives put a high value on that. But they have to pay peanuts for it – and as I say, I think it's probably the case that the musicians get nothing at all.]

Not only that, but it really is <u>so rare</u> that cafes and coffee shops put on live music. I know that even very competent "local" musicians often have very few opportunities to perform, and it would be so much better if cafes and coffee shops "routinely" put on performers – and paid them a decent amount of money.

C) All The Spoils Go To The Top 5% (Or Less)

It came as a surprise to me that at The Lights (which is quite a small theatre/entertainment centre), some of the acts could be described as "world class". In fact, most of the acts have something that really "sets them apart" - perhaps, if it's rock for instance, they were famous 20 or 30 years ago.

Now, if we think of there being a "hierarchy" of venues, I don't think there can be all that much existing in the very considerable gulf between a 250 – 300 seat theatre set-up such as the Lights, and the pub venues – simply because a set-up like the Lights probably has to be at least that size to be financially viable at all. (However it would be possible for a much smaller theatre set-up to exist that concentrated on one-man performances – this is what The Forge in Basingstoke does [attached to the Anvil, and only about 100 seats.)

And when one thinks of pub venues where I believe bands are typically paid about £150, the musicians can't be earning hardly anything at all once they've paid their expenses.

In fact, this seems a good place to put one of my "articles within an article". (The appalling way we treat "pub musicians")

Article Within An Article (A)
The appalling way we treat "pub musicians"

Where I live (and probably in most towns of a fair size), almost every weekend, there are at least 3 or 4 local bands performing live in pubs.

It seems to be "standard" that there is free admission. Almost always the pubs attract more customers on the nights they have these bands, and so sell more drink, and the band are paid out of the increased profit the landlord makes from selling this. But this almost always puts a very low limit on what the band is paid. I think the "going rate" is about £150 in most towns.

But a typical band will have quite high expenses, and probably this means that if, say, the band has 4 members, each will come away with maybe £25 if they're lucky. I think that's appalling.

The amount of training even a fairly ordinary pub musician does is usually immense. A couple who lived next door to my parents for many years had a son who was learning the guitar. It seemed that whenever I went round my parents' house this boy was practising his music (I learnt that later he was in a band). Exactly the same – near where I live there's someone learning the drums. And a very high percentage of times that I pass that house (at various times of the day), I can hear the drums going. I wouldn't be surprised if both these boys put in an average of 3 hours practice a day – for years and years. And many musicians start very young.

I'd say if you total it all up most of these musicians have spent a lot more time practising than, say, most people spend studying for a degree.

And then, when they've "made it" and play in a band, regularly attracting a very enthusiastic and sizeable audience (maybe), they can expect possibly £20 for a 2-hour performance, which when you take rehearsals into account, is probably much less than the minimum wage!

I can't for the life of me see why it isn't "standard" that you pay an average of £5, maybe, to see a band in a pub, that the band should receive all the entrance fees received in most cases; and that they should still attract a sizeable crowd (if competent); that a band might then typically receive more like £500 for a gig. That seems to me to be what should be the case, and I cannot really understand why it isn't.

PS I'm not really blaming the landlords, by the way. No doubt a lot of them have tried making an admission charge of around £5 but have nearly always seen the numbers go right down. Rather, I have to put the blame on the public, who are seemingly quite willing to pay a tradesman £60 or more for a 10-minute job like repairing a tap, but apparently unwilling to pay £5 to see (a 2-hour performance by) a rock group.

....

Therefore, from what I've said above (that "article within an article" and the few paragraphs before it), it means that the only people making a living from their music, are those playing venues like The Lights, or bigger places (with the possible exception of lone performers).

And these, as I think I've implied (by saying that a lot of them are practically world class) are actually probably in the top 2% of musicians, not just the top 5%.

....

I was watching X-Factor once, and one of the judges was commenting on the performance of a young man who had just sung, who had made it to the top 4 or 5 of the show.

She was being extremely enthusiastic about his performance – full of superlatives, and then said (which seemed strange to me) that he might actually have a career in this to look forward to. And I don't think she was being ironic at all. That was exactly what she meant – that he might (if he was lucky) have a career in music, and he might not.

Now, about 10,000 people enter X-Factor each year, I think, and I know that some of them are dreadful, but surely a reasonable proportion must really take their singing seriously, practice a lot, and be quite competent – perhaps a fifth, shall we say? That's 2000 people. And this judge has said that this person, who has made it to the top 4 <u>might</u> have a career!

Just imagine if, out of 2000 students studying engineering at university, only 4 or 5 found work in it, or out of 2000 students doing a law degree, only 4 or 5 made it as solicitors! (There would be a bit of an outcry, wouldn't there?)

(4 out of 2000 is not 5%, not 2%, but 0.2%!)

ARTICLE 11

Slaves To The Methodist Work Ethic – Why Many People Work Too Hard

Note: This next article (mostly) describes a period of self-employment. This article was written about 10 years ago.

Quite a long time ago I was a salesman. Believe it or not I usually only got 2 appointments (selling situations) a week. Fortunately, I was a very good salesman once I had the appointment, so I very often made 2 sales a week too, which was enough to make a living (it was commission only).

I was generally with the couple (for some reason I rarely had appointments with single men or women), about an hour and a half for the appointment, so that was usually 3 hours of my week taken up.

All the rest of my working week (apart from the travelling) was free for "prospecting" - a selling person's term for "getting appointments".

I usually spent 3 or 4 hours a day doing this. But in fact, possibly due to the nature of the product, virtually all this "prospecting" I did was a dead loss. Nine tenths of my appointments came by way of someone who lived in my sales area enquiring, having seen one of the firm's adverts.

I would have earned 90% as much if I didn't do any of the prospecting, but just waited for responses to the advertising – in other words if I just worked 3 hours a week. But, in fact, I was working more or less full time.

I was "a slave to the Methodist work ethic" – that's how I'm defining the term, for my purposes.

I did improve, in that respect, as time went on, however – for example, when I ran an introduction agency quite a few years later.

(This was before any of the internet-based social networking sites, and before internet dating became at all popular. I don't suppose firms like the one I ran hardly exist anymore – but they were commonplace about 15 years ago or so.)

It wasn't that I had a thing about the "singles" scene, particularly, but I didn't have much capital, didn't want to take on office premises, didn't want to have to buy lots of stock, and didn't have any engineering training (much self-employed work is based on one or other of the engineering trades). And with all these "didn't want to's" there really were very few options remaining (that I could think of, anyway).

The income I made from this business wasn't great. I cannot claim that it was very financially successful.

But in another respect, I think I can pat myself on the back a little bit and claim to have been successful. That is, I believe I managed to do effectively the same work that many agencies with a similar number of members did, but by "putting in" very few hours. Usually, I was only working at the business for 6 or 7 hours a week, whereas some of these other agencies actually had several full-time employees – the difference was that marked.

And in this article I want to concentrate on that aspect – being successful at "getting the work done" with really very little effort.

Anyway – first, the big picture.

I built up the membership to about 1400, and I believe just about all these members had the opportunity to meet anyone else on the register that they were likely to be suited to – surely an introduction agency can't really do more than that, at the end of the day. (I'm not saying everyone <u>did</u> meet all members they might have been suited to, of course. I'm saying that if they wrote in several times, with reasonable time gaps between, they would have been "introduced" to virtually all the possibly suitable members on my database – within a certain travelling distance, of course.)

And yet, as stated above, I was really putting in only about 6 or 7 hours work a week in total.

I'm not going to give a full running commentary on how I ran the business. But I'll mention a few of the things I did which caused the workload to be so light.

After I have done this (in some detail), I will try to summarise the "lessons learnt", that might well be relevant to many other firms (even much bigger ones, perhaps) – suggesting how firms might also lighten their workload.

First of all, unless I was expecting a phone call at a particular time, I always used an answerphone.

I was getting certainly less than 10 enquiries a day for nearly all the time I was running the agency, and I certainly didn't want to man the phone continuously for those few calls.

(Typically, about one in five of the enquirers would join.

The reason I had 1400 members was because quite a lot of people stayed members for more than a year.)

All my adverts had (24hrs) printed after the telephone number, so people knew they were going to get an answerphone. Maybe this would only apply to a few businesses, but I'm convinced I got more calls because of this rather than less. People are a bit embarrassed about joining an introduction agency and would rather ring an answerphone than staff at the agency. That's what I always felt. In fact, I noticed that the relatively few times I did take the call personally, there was a considerably greater chance of "losing" the enquiry (for some reason not getting a name and address) than if it went through the answerphone.

In contrast, I think most other agencies (e.g. most of the type of agency I contrasted myself with above) would man the phone(s) certainly all day anyway. It is enormously expensive to man a phone all day if you are only getting a few enquiries a day, and I'm convinced that a very large number of small firms do only get a few (serious) enquiries a day.

I'll just say something else about this. Obviously with it being an answerphone, people could choose when to ring, and it was noticeable that nearly everyone rang in the evening, between about 6pm and 9pm. And yet very many firms (who deal with the general public) will man the phone during office hours, but not even have an answerphone in the evening.

I would deal with the enquiries in a batch every two or three days. It only took about an hour or so to do this.

I sometimes dealt with the new memberships as they came in, or else again in batches every few days. It really didn't involve much work. It was all computerised, of course. Using a database program, I could easily arrange for details of anyone on the register likely to be suitable to be printed out – it was only a job of a few minutes to set up the person's record and do this. The details included the person's contact details, their age, occupation, a list of interests and maybe a little more information which I forget. It was much more information than a lot of agencies gave.

I would simply send these off with a short, standard, covering letter.

When/if they wrote asking for more introductions at a later date it was even easier – exactly the same process except this time I wouldn't need to input the record.

(You just had to put the date of the last time they had a list in a certain box, to make sure they only got details of people who had joined since then.)

That was really the main part of the work I did. I think a lot of agencies did an awful lot more work, but I fail to see why that is necessary. For instance, they would chase people up who didn't join with several follow-up letters. When they made an introduction, they would maybe phone the person and try to "sell" the idea of them making contact with their introduction, then they would phone them up again a week or so later to see if they had. Then they would contact them yet again to see how the date went etc. I really don't see that all that is necessary, but obviously if you do that it is a hell of a lot more work – but what does it really gain?

Other agencies often committed themselves to sending new introduction lists every 3 months, or even every month, but again I didn't do that. I felt that quite a high percentage of people who joined found when it came to it that they were too shy, or didn't have the bottle to contact their introductions, and I would likely not hear from them again – it would have been sheer waste of time to send them new lists every month, which would have gone straight in the bin. (But 9 times out of 10 they wouldn't cancel their membership – I think they were still pleased to be contacted by other members.). Obviously if I had committed to send everyone a new list every month, it would have been enormously more time consuming. I would almost certainly have needed staff.

Those, then, are some of the differences between my agency and others – why some agencies with fewer members needed 7 or 8 full time staff perhaps. But to me it would be an example of being "a slave to the Methodist work ethic".

I won't say any more about this business. What I'll come onto now is the fact that over the years I've been plagued with a seemingly continual avalanche of mail from quite a few firms (some very well known) who thus prove themselves to be "slaves to the Methodist work ethic".

The one I'll talk about is NTL (the cable TV company)

Actually, I hardly watch TV at all. I don't find it at all relaxing, or stimulating, come to that. I'd really rather listen to music.

But for well over a year (if I remember rightly), I was getting quite an expensive looking mailing piece advertising NTL, I'm sure about once a month, and of course they all went straight in the bin.

Now, okay, I'm sure NTL can justify this sort of expenditure. They can say something like "Once someone subscribes to us, they're likely to stay with us for years, spending £40 a month or whatever, so it's worth us spending £20 on each household if necessary, if they've got a 1 in 5 chance of taking up the service." - or something like that.

So, looked at that way, I suppose you can say – yes, it's justified.

But there's just something that niggles me about it all. It's like this.

In some ways so much is expected of everyone these days. As if everyone is thought to be so bright. It is believed that half the adolescent population ought to go to university, for instance – and most university textbooks are really not easy going at all.

Another thing – sometimes I think I ought to get a "normal" job of some kind, and I look through the local paper at the job vacancies. And – don't you agree? - all the jobs on offer sound incredibly complicated. I tend to look through them and think "I don't know that I could do that" to most of them.

And these are often quite low paid jobs. And yet about 95% of the population are employed, mostly in jobs with higher salaries than these.

So – in various ways the average person is thought to be so "capable". [I've given two examples and could give more.]

167

But surely, if everyone is so capable, then they are at least able to successfully make the following decision and do the necessary information gathering:-

"Let's see, do I want satellite television?"

[Answer yes, no or don't know.]

If yes or don't know, look into what's on offer.

Looking into what's on offer is surely very easy – there are only basically two main companies (in this area) – Sky and NTL, so it's simply a question of finding out what each of them offers. Then deciding between the two.

(I'd certainly agree that Sky and NTL should make it easy for people to find out what they offer.)

I just think it's an insult to people's intelligence to apparently assume that they're not capable of making the above thought processes/taking appropriate action.

By my reasoning, NTL might just as well take out a smallish ad in each edition of the Yellow Pages (total cost: no more than £70,000 a year probably), rather than spend however much it costs to send an expensive mailing piece to millions of homes once a month!

You know, I read a lot of marketing books a few years ago, and there was this idea in a lot of them that everyone is a marketer these days.

And I've been thinking about this, and some strange thoughts have come to me.

I have this idea (it's sort of half a joke and half serious), that in a business there's only really 2 things – making whatever you make (or providing whatever service you offer), and marketing it.

And that these days, because the manufacture of most things can be automated (or the item can be bought from India or China for a very low amount), the division is something like 10% of the money making the product (or buying it from India or China), and 90% of the money marketing it!

But how is all the money wasted?

I'm not qualified to say in very many parts of a business. But thinking about it, on the other hand, perhaps I do have something useful to say...

I realise that running an introduction agency is a relatively simple thing to do (which was one of the things that attracted me to it).

But perhaps it can be considered to be a kind of microcosm, or a simplified representation of what happens in a much bigger firm.

And maybe bigger firms can learn something from the ways I, in my situation, was able to reduce my workload so greatly compared to other introduction agencies I contrasted mine with.

And it seems to me that there were basically 3 things the contrasting organisations did that I didn't do.

A) Chasing Potential Customers For The Order (Or Membership Fee).

As I said I just sent people the brochure or sales letter in response to the initial enquiry, then left them alone after that. If they didn't join, they didn't join. I accepted it.

In contrast some of these other organisations sent people who enquired once, countless letters with new "offers" over a period of several years sometimes. I know this because I enquired to quite a few of these other agencies to get an idea of what "the competition" was like – and in some cases I am still getting the occasional letter from them over 10 years later! And of course, to send 10 letters costs ten times as much as to send one.

B) "Nannying" Customers

I mentioned that some of these other agencies would ring their members every time they sent them an introduction and try to "sell" them the idea of making contact, then maybe make a couple of phone calls to see if they had done so, then phone again after a date to see how it went etc. Of course, all this represents an enormous amount of work. I never did any of it.

I am calling this "nannying" customers. I'm sure it has an equivalent in a lot of firms. Perhaps those firms would increase their efficiency by reducing it, or even cutting it out altogether.

C) Being At Customers' Beck And Call / Waiting On Them

The example I am giving of this is having a phone manned all the time waiting for enquiry calls, whereas I'm sure a lot of small firms have relatively few (serious) enquiry sales calls. Sometimes only literally a very few a week – I bet 8 or 9 a week isn't all that uncommon.

....

As I said, I'm sure there are many equivalents to these 3 "inefficiencies" in many firms. My feeling is that it would be a particularly good idea for many firms to stop chasing customers – just make information about the products easily available and customers might well come of their own accord, and the firm's overheads might be reduced immensely, enabling prices to be lower than competitors. In any event, firms ought to pay people the compliment that they think they are intelligent enough to be able to decide whether or not they want something, having been made aware of it maybe just the once.

Here is a sample article from the 'sister book' to this one – 'Mainly about conquering sexual repression'.

Eureka

As a young man, I found that when I didn't have a girlfriend, I often was unable to make much of an impression on new girls that I met – not so much as I had done when I had a partner.

I'm sure it was due to sexual repression. Therefore I think that, especially when one is without a girlfriend, one needs to see what one can do to combat this.

(I'll talk from the point of view of men) – and give a little bit of defence of (or indeed some praise and recommendation of) 'erotica'.

Surely, to be heterosexual, partly means that we find a good looking woman who is naked very attractive in some way.

About the best way that I can define the phrase 'sex-phobic' (analogous to aggression-phobic as described elsewhere in my writing) is to say that it is a denial of that.

And I am going to say that just as those in the encounter group movement of the eighties thought we had an aggression-phobic society, it could be said that today we have a very sex-phobic one.

Of course, there have always been a lot of people – for example, religious people – who have thought that women should be 'modest'. There have always been a lot of people who have very much looked down on glamour models, for instance.

But when I say that we are becoming very much a 'sex-phobic' society, I am going much further than acknowledging that. Very much further indeed.

I can't quite say in one paragraph, really, exactly what I mean. All I can do is give a few examples. Everything is relative – and I shall quite often compare 'the situation' as I see it now, with what it was like, as I remember it, about 25 years ago.

Until about 20 years ago, I was quite religious and felt very guilty about anything in the way of 'erotica', but after I rejected Christianity, felt that guilt no more.

I bought a few girlie magazines first of all, and these helped to relax me – made me feel less tense – in other words helped me feel much better.

But eventually, wanting some 'real live action', I decided to go to a strip club in London. Probably the main reason why I didn't make this decision sooner was my finances. I've always hated staying in the whole evening and watching television or whatever, but I knew that if I went to London, even once a fortnight, it would come to that quite often (because I wasn't very well off).

But anyway, in the end I decided to go – to hell with the financial consequences.

The only place I had heard of was Raymond's Revue Bar – it had been advertised – a full back page advert sometimes, in one of the girlie magazines I bought.

Also, I had read an article about it once which I was sure had mentioned that there were afternoon performances.

So I decided to go on a Thursday afternoon. Obviously it didn't really matter to me what performance I went to, and I thought it would be easier to get a ticket for an afternoon performance.

When I got there about 1.30, the place was all shut up. I found out that there were 2 performances a day – 8pm and 10pm. Also that the box office didn't open till 5pm.

My hopes sank quite a bit, actually. I thought it was unlikely that I'd get a ticket. But I decided to go along when the box office opened anyway.
I had taken quite a lot of money, and I went to a local pub and had maybe 3 drinks, though a couple of them were cokes, for obvious reasons.

I needn't have worried about ticket availability at all. When I got to the box office just after 5, the man asked me if I wanted a front-row seat.

I decided to take a seat 3 or 4 rows back – they were a bit less expensive. But I was very surprised that I had the chance of practically any seat I wanted – and I hadn't even expected to get a seat at all. Bear in mind that Raymond's Revue Bar is one of the most famous strip clubs in the world.
So anyway, back to the pub for a couple more drinks (the seat I bought was £20, or maybe £25, by the way).

I went back to the Revue Bar about 25 minutes before the performance was due to start – I was probably the first or second person there.

The music was good – quite loud, and I began to get quite excited with the anticipation. It was the first time I'd done anything like this.

I ordered a drink – served by a waiter. It was a bit more expensive than a pub, but not exorbitant (about £3.50 for a bottle of Budweiser, I think) – I had been used to nightclubs charging well over double pub prices for drinks when in my twenties – so I was actually quite pleasantly surprised.

More people arrived in the next quarter of an hour or so, of course, but really not that many.

The performance started about a quarter of an hour late (as I came to discover was normal). I'm not really good at describing things like that – the performance, I mean – it's not the kind of writing I'm best at.

But it was stunning. Those girls – there were about 7 of them – were gorgeous. I had very rarely seen such beautiful women.

Though I am certainly no expert at all, they all seemed very talented dancers to me. (There was one man too, by the way – I was to find out that there were quite often a few women in the audience.)

The costumes were amazing too – though for quite a lot of the time – much more time than I had dared hope, the girls were effectively naked.

(Incidentally, there was quite a bit of 'aggression' in some of the dancing too.)

I suppose the total performance time, compared to, say, a 'normal' West End theatre, wasn't that great. The performance was over just after 9.30 and there was about a 10 minute interval – so I suppose the performance time wasn't much more than an hour.

But when you think that for a significant amount of it you've got 2 or 3 girls perhaps – sometimes all the dancers, dancing very provocatively without a stitch on, just a few feet away from you – well I had no complaints at all, I thought it was incredible value.

But the crazy thing was that there couldn't have been more than 30 or 40 customers. And there never really were many more than that – which meant that the theatre was just about always only a quarter full or less – though I suppose the later performance might well have been busier. But I just couldn't understand it at all. (Also a high percentage of them tended to be foreign – obviously tourists – quite a lot were Japanese, I think. There really were very few ordinary British people indeed.)

(I am sure that 15 years before this, a place like this would have been jam-packed nearly every night.)

So – I very greatly enjoyed my first visit to Raymond's Revue Bar – but the best thing about it was still to come.

This was because the next day I felt like a new man. I hadn't felt so good in many years. My friends, especially the regulars at the pub I went to about 3 times a week, noticed the difference too. Overnight I became more confident and less tense.

I want to come back later and say something about the reaction of the people I knew (especially those in the pub), to what I told them.

Going back now to say something about there being so few customers at Raymond's Revue Bar.

I just couldn't believe it, to be honest, and here's why. I hadn't at this time really been a part of a large group of maybe a dozen men, socialising together, for some while. But at one time it was quite common (eg after football training). And I always felt that I had quite good insight – that I could 'suss people out' quite well.

Anyway, suppose, then, that I was amongst this group of about a dozen men, in a pub after football training, say. And suppose that the question was put to us, that we could either go to a strip club show like the one I've just described, or to a top level football match – my instinct would be that it would be about half and half – half a dozen would like the idea of the strip club, and the others the football. That would be my guess.

And what I couldn't get my head round at all, was the fact that it appeared this guess was so inaccurate.

It is true that during the period I was going to Raymond's Revue Bar, its star was falling – it was in a bit of a decline (and I understand it closed down just a few years later). Also these stage performances were not its principal activity anymore – it turned into a lap dancing club called *Amazons* at 11.30 pm until about 4 am, I believe. And I think that format for a strip club (although outside my price range – you could get through several hundred pounds of a night) had become more popular than the stage shows it was replacing.

Nevertheless I was still surprised at this very low turnout (that it was not more than a quarter full) at these superb stage performances, at this very famous club, and I couldn't help but compare it with the vast stadiums filled to capacity, which top level football matches often achieve.

Going back to when I mentioned to the regulars at my local about having been to a strip club. The change in me because of this experience must have been obvious to them. You would have thought that they would be pleased for me that I had found something that 'suited me' – that made me feel good.

Not a bit of it.

I chose mainly to tell the people there about this when there might have been a group of men, a couple of them telling a few dirty jokes – it happened quite frequently. They often would be laughing like mad at really quite crude jokes. Fair enough, I've never been one to complain about an off-colour joke – but I was really surprised that the reaction of these same people, when I told them that I had seen real strippers doing their stuff, was very subdued. It all went a bit quiet, and I realised that I had made a bit of a faux pas.

I soon learned not to mention my trips to Raymond's Revue Bar.
And I really found this hypocritical, that they would laugh so enthusiastically at a few dirty jokes, but go all quiet – obviously disapproving – when I told them I had been to a strip club.

I said I was going to compare the situation with how I remembered it quite a few years before.

I never got round to going to a strip club in my twenties – my religious views at the time more or less precluded it.

But I did get sent on a computer course in London with about 12 colleagues, and one night we all went round Soho.

Everyone (as I remember it) was quite excitedly looking at what was on offer (from outside the various premises). I was very disappointed that no-one could reach any agreement about actually paying an entrance fee and venturing inside one of these 'dens of iniquity'. (On spur of the moment things like this I could sometimes suspend my religious principles and I probably would have enthusiastically ventured in, if only a consensus to do so had been reached.)

But anyway, as I say, everyone was fairly excitedly discussing the possibility of going in somewhere. And supposing a couple of us had gone off and been less 'stick in the mud' – then I'm sure the reaction of the majority – when the pair of us came back to report, wouldn't have been nearly so negative as I had found that many years later – I'm convinced that attitudes had changed dramatically in the intervening years.

I carried on going to Raymond's Revue Bar, usually every fortnight, for some while. Then I got to hear that one of the pubs in my home town (the Swan) had 'exotic dancers' on a Tuesday and a Sunday.

I later found out that 'exotic dancers' was another term for strippers really, probably preferred by the girls themselves. At the time I didn't quite know what it meant – I thought it possible they might take everything off, but wasn't sure.

After a few weeks I decided to go along to the Swan at one of these sessions – it was a Sunday afternoon and by this time the Tuesday evenings had already been cancelled.

Again, as with Raymond's Revue Bar, I was very pleasantly surprised by the experience. The girls (there were four of them each week) were all very attractive, and they did indeed take everything off.

Sometimes they didn't have much to take off. When one girl stripped off her dress to reveal she had nothing further to take off, I was amused to hear the bloke by the side of me say "I think they ought to wear knickers!"
The girls would come round and talk to you individually, while they were dancing, even when they were naked, and I found that a great turn-on. I even had one quite long conversation with a girl – and her without a stitch on!

They would take it in turns to do a dance to a pop record, about every 10 minutes. You put a pound in a pint glass the girl carried round before each dance.

I took about £35 with me I think, and as it turned out, my money did last virtually the whole afternoon – 2pm to 6pm (and including a few drinks). Again I considered this incredible value.

And again I was very surprised at the relative lack of response, and lack of enthusiasm really, at all this.

I got the impression that a lot of people thought it was a bit 'overpriced' – that to pay a pound for each and every dance was a bit much. One or two people said just that.

Hardly any of the regulars seemed to be interested. And you wouldn't call it an 'upmarket' pub at all. Quite a high percentage of them (the men), I would say, consider themselves sort of 'Jack the lad' type personalities, boasting about their ability to drink gallons on occasion etc etc. But when it came down to it almost all of them 'retired' to the other bar when the real action began.

A few watched for a brief period of maybe 20 minutes before 'retiring', but I can't remember very many watching for an extended period.

There were quite a few people in the bar where the girls were dancing, I'm not saying it was quiet, but most, I think, came from a few miles away – the sessions had been advertised in the local paper.

But even they didn't stay all that long. I think I was virtually the only one who would come at 2 (when it started) and stay till it finished at 6. Typically, the others would be there maybe an hour and a half. I couldn't imagine what they had to do that was so much more enticing than what was on offer at the Swan.

I only went to about 3 or 4 of these performances. When I went along after that I found they had been cancelled.

I never did get to find out why. One of the bar staff told me it was because one of the customers had been rude to one of the girls and the landlord hadn't taken strong enough action (i.e. evicted him), and the girls had refused to come back.

It sounded reasonable and I accepted it at the time. But I had been at the last performance and hadn't seen any trouble.

I now think it more likely that the landlord had suddenly realised that people were talking behind his back, perhaps – that whereas he had been very well liked – he was a very sociable sort of person – now a sizeable proportion of the customers were 'looking down on him' for putting on shows like this and his reputation had suffered, rather than been enhanced. (Just as I had been looked down on when I admitted having been to a strip club by the regulars at my local.)

In fact it wasn't too long after that that the landlord and his wife sold up and moved elsewhere. They hadn't been there that long and there were rumours that they'd put a lot of money into the pub, and I'm sure they had originally intended to stay much longer.

It may well have been because they felt they still hadn't been 'forgiven' for having these strippers. Of course all this is speculation on my part, but I wouldn't be surprised if that's what actually happened.

…..(continuing)

I can understand very religious people being negative about these things – but the negativity about it seems to affect over 90% of men these days, not just the religious.

But this denial (that men are interested in seeing naked women) – which I'm describing as being sex-phobic (analogous to being aggression-phobic as I have written about elsewhere) I don't think is very good for people at all.

To me, most men in particular, even quite young men, seem not so 'emotionally alive' – haven't got so much 'life force' as I remember men of the same age, back 25 or so years ago. And I wouldn't be at all surprised if the epidemic I've called 'sex-phobic' is largely responsible for that.

PS   These experiences at Raymond's Revue Bar and The Swan happened quite a few years ago now – and Raymond's Revue Bar closed down several years ago.